Leckie
the education publisher
for Scotland

National 5
ENGLISH

For exams from 2026

Student Book

Simon Hall

Published by Leckie
An imprint of HarperCollins Publishers
1 Robroyston Gate,
Glasgow
G33 1JN

leckiescotland@harpercollins.co.uk
leckiescotland.co.uk

HarperCollins Publishers
Macken House
39/40 Mayor Street Upper
Dublin 1
D01 C9W8
Ireland

First Edition 2026

10 9 8 7 6 5 4 3 2 1

© HarperCollins Publishers 2026

ISBN 9780008774691

Printed in the UK by Martins the Printers

Author: Simon Hall
Managing Editor: Julianna Dunn
For the Publisher: Gillian Bowman, Clare Souza
Design: Sarah Duxbury, Ian Wrigley
Typesetter: Six Red Marbles Ltd

Acknowledgements

Extracts
'Trouble is not my middle name' by Liz Lochhead on p68 is reproduced by permission of Birlinn Ltd, with permission of the licensor through PLS clear; 'We lost us for a while' by Robert Alan Jamieson on p71 is reproduced by permission of Taproot Press UK; *Yellow Moon* by David Greig is reproduced by permission of Faber & Faber; *Sailmaker* by Alan Spence on p87 is reproduced by permission of Hodder and Stoughton Educational Ltd © 1988, Alan Spence, with permission of the licensor through PLS clear; *Tally's Blood* by Ann Marie Di Mambro on p90 is reproduced by permission of Hodder Education © 2002, with permission of the licensor through PLS clear; *The Strange Case of Dr Jekyll and Mr Hyde* by Robert Louis Stevenson on p101 is in the public domain; *Duck Feet* by Ely Percy on p104 is reproduced by permission of Monstrous Regiment Publishing Ltd / Leith Books; *All That Glisters* from *Hieroglyphics and other stories* by Anne Donavan on p106 is reproduced by permission of Canongate Books © 2001, with permission of the licensor through PLS clear; *Death in a Nut* as told by Duncan Williamson on p108 is in the public domain; 'Medusa' by Carol Ann Duffy on page 120, published in *The World's Wife* by Anvil Press Poetry, 1999. Copyright © Carol Ann Duffy; 'Old Highland Woman' by Norman MacCaig on p123 is reproduced by permission of Birlinn Ltd, with permission of the licensor through PLS clear; 'Gap Year' from *Darling: New & Selected Poems* by Jackie Kay on p125 is reproduced by permission of Bloodaxe Books, on behalf of the publisher www.bloodaxebooks.com; 'Love' from *Love and a Life* by Edwin Morgan on p127 is reproduced by permission of Carcanet Press, 'Little Girls' from *Poyums* by Len Pennie is reproduced by permission of Canongate Books, with permission of the licensor through PLS clear.

Images
P15: Sharaf Maksumov/Alamy; p16: Mike Clark/Alamy; p19: Laurie Campbell/Alamy; p25: Andrew Greaves/Alamy; p43: imageBROKER.com/Alamy; p50: Peter Devlin/Alamy; p57: Cernan Elias/Alamy; p68: Cavan Images/Alamy; p85: drew farrell/Alamy; p89: World History Archive/Alamy; p90: Elizabeth Leyden/Alamy; p167: David Hall; p172: Rob Watkins/Alamy

All other images © Shutterstock.com

FSC
www.fsc.org

MIX
Paper | Supporting
responsible forestry
FSC™ C013254

Contents

Introduction	5
Welcome to your National 5 English Student Book	5

Part 1   Reading for Understanding, Analysis and Evaluation   6

Reading for Understanding, Analysis and Evaluation: What is it?		6
Reading for Understanding, Analysis and Evaluation: How to do it		9
1	'Using your own words' questions	9
2	'Examples of language' questions – word choice	15
3	'Examples of language' questions – imagery	19
4	'Examples of language' questions – sentence structure	23
5	A note on 'examples of language'	31
6	Questions that ask you to explain 'links' in the text	32
7	Implication	35
8	Questions that ask you to 'summarise'	35
9	Questions that ask you about the 'effectiveness of the passage's conclusion'	38
Example Question Paper 1 – *Just Grow Up!*		42
Model Answers 1 – *Just Grow Up!*		46
Example Question Paper 2 – *Get Myself Connected*		49
Model Answers 2 – *Get Myself Connected*		53
Example Question Paper 3 – *Egg Terrorists*		56
Model Answers 3 – *Egg Terrorists*		60

Part 2   Critical Reading   63

Critical Reading: What is it?		63
1	Section 1: Scottish texts	63
2	Section 2: Critical essay	64
Critical Reading: How to do it		67
1	Section 1: Scottish texts	67
2	Section 2: Critical essay	75
3	Study tips and advice on how to prepare for Critical Reading	81
Section 1: Scottish Texts – Example Question Paper and Model Answers		83
	Drama: *Yellow Moon* by David Greig	83
	Drama: *Sailmaker* by Alan Spence	87
	Drama: *Tally's Blood* by Ann Marie Di Mambro	90

Prose:	*The Strange Case of Dr Jekyll and Mr Hyde* by Robert Louis Stevenson	101
Prose:	*Duck Feet* by Ely Percy	104
Prose:	*All That Glisters* by Anne Donovan, plus references to *Hieroglyphics*	106
Prose:	Scottish short stories: *Death in a Nut* as told by Duncan Williamson, plus references to *Things My Wife and I Found Hidden in Our House* by Kirsty Logan	108
Poetry:	'Medusa' by Carol Ann Duffy, plus references to 'Mrs Midas'	120
Poetry:	'Old Highland Woman' by Norman MacCaig, plus references to 'Aunt Julia'	123
Poetry:	'Gap Year' by Jackie Kay, plus references to 'Keeping Orchids'	125
Poetry:	'Love' by Edwin Morgan, plus references to 'Strawberries'	127
Poetry:	'Little Girls' by Len Pennie, plus references to 'A Red, Red Rose' by Robert Burns	129

Section 2: Critical Essay – Example Essays		145
1	Drama – *Black Watch* by Gregory Burke	145
2	Prose – *To Kill a Mockingbird* by Harper Lee	147
3	Poetry – 'Trio' by Edwin Morgan	149

Part 3   Performance – Spoken Language   151

Performance – Spoken Language: What is it?	151
Performance – Spoken Language: How to do it	153

Part 4   Portfolio Writing   155

Portfolio Writing: What is it?		155
Portfolio Writing: How to do it		158
1	Success criteria for portfolio writing	158
2	Advice for portfolio writing	159
Example Portfolio Writing – Discursive (argumentative): *Renewable Revolution*		162
Commentary on *Renewable Revolution*		164
Example Portfolio Writing – Creative (personal/reflective): *Diamond*		166
Commentary on *Diamond*		167
Example Portfolio Writing – Creative (short story): *Swiftly Past the Thieves' Isle*		169
Commentary on *Swiftly Past the Thieves' Isle*		171
Glossary		173
Index		175

Introduction

Welcome to your *National 5 English Student Book*

Your *National 5 English Student Book* draws on up-to-date educational thinking and reflects the latest changes to the National 5 English course and Scottish texts. It provides the most useful material to prepare you for your National 5 English exam, spoken language assessment and portfolio writing. It explains what each part of the course involves and provides specimen paper practice materials and examples, as well as a rich range of model answers. If you use this book well, and take time to study it, it will help you to reach the very best grade you can in National 5 English.

The example passages for Reading for Understanding, Analysis and Evaluation (RUAE) and portfolio writing included in this book make the most of links to other subject areas across the curriculum, such as sciences, music, history, sport and the environment. Your *National 5 English Student Book* is specially written for learners in Scottish schools and sets National 5 English firmly within a recognisable Scottish context. We hope you will enjoy studying with this guide, and we wish you all the very best with your National 5 English course.

Part 1

Reading for Understanding, Analysis and Evaluation

Reading for Understanding, Analysis and Evaluation: What is it?

RUAE stands for Reading for Understanding, Analysis and Evaluation. In this part of the course, you will be working to develop your skills in **reading**.

RUAE focuses on your reading of **non-fiction**. So, the texts you study will be about factual topics, as opposed to the imaginative or fictional texts you will study in the Critical Reading Scottish text and Critical Essay parts of your course.

In the examination, you will read a **previously unseen** passage, and answer questions about it.

The text chosen for the National 5 examination paper is carefully selected to ensure that the subject matter is interesting for young people. The topic of the passage will be engaging and relevant. The passage often focuses on something that young people will already be interested in or something they will have some knowledge of. Passages in recent years have focused on aspects of popular contemporary topics such as gaming, music and online culture.

Although the topics of the RUAE texts are factual, you should be aware that the texts will also include the writer's personal views within a developed 'argument' – an extended and developing opinion or persuasive idea that runs through the passage. This combination of factual material with the writer's personal views woven through generally makes for an interesting read.

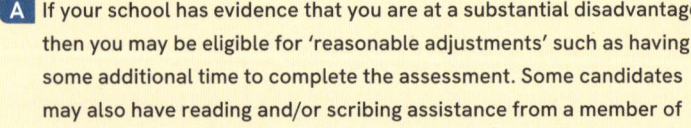

Candidate question

I have dyslexia, and I find the reading process really challenging. Are there ways my school can help to make RUAE fair for me?

A If your school has evidence that you are at a substantial disadvantage then you may be eligible for 'reasonable adjustments' such as having some additional time to complete the assessment. Some candidates may also have reading and/or scribing assistance from a member of staff. You should speak to teachers in your school about this.

The selected passage is always very well written, and you will find it stimulating and entertaining. Often the passage will relate to other parts of the curriculum or other subjects you may be studying.

Studying RUAE presents you with an excellent opportunity to develop sophisticated skills in reading. Developing your ability to understand, analyse and evaluate written language is key not only for accessing your wider curriculum, but also to your future lifelong learning.

RUAE will test and challenge you by asking you to do the following things:

- engage with, consider and select the main details of a text
- identify and select detailed information from a text
- analyse and evaluate a writer's choice and use of language
- evaluate the overall effects and impact of a text.

The examination question paper for RUAE consists of a passage approximately 1,000 words long, followed by a series of approximately nine questions. A short, italicised introductory sentence will give you some background information and lead you into the passage itself. Take care not to overlook this introductory sentence; most people find it very useful.

Once you have read the passage, the questions test a predictable range of your skills. Some questions focus on your understanding, while others ask you to analyse specific language techniques the writer has used. Some questions may ask you to evaluate how effective the writing is, or how well the writer has communicated their point of view or line of argument. There is often a question asking how effectively you feel the writer has concluded or finished the passage. You will learn about each of the different question types in the *RUAE: How to do it* section of this book.

TOP TIP

When you begin working on RUAE, the passages may seem more challenging than any reading you have done in the past. Don't worry – most people have exactly the same experience! Stay calm and read carefully and methodically. Re-read if you need to.

Candidate question

Is 1,000 words a lot? What do 1,000 words look like on the page?

A 1,000 words cover about one and a half pages of A4 in 12-point font size.

Written text is an amazing thing. It enables a writer to communicate thoughts and ideas to a reader, who then uses their own skills and experiences to create a meaning or a 'reading' of the text.

Candidate question

Should I read the whole passage before I begin to think about the questions?

A Yes, you should read the passage in full, as quickly as you can without sacrificing your accuracy. As you read through, as well as making sense of the writer's language, you will be evaluating the writer's point of view on the topic. It will be very useful for you to start thinking about the writer's stance or opinion from the moment you begin reading. Broadly, does the writer feel positive or negative about the subject matter of the passage? How do you know? Does the writer's stance shift at all as the passage progresses?

You will probably already have experience of doing this kind of reading work during the upper stages of primary school and through your early years of secondary school. Developing ever more sophisticated skills in reading as you study this part of your National 5 course will challenge you, but it will also begin to open your mind to new ideas and new ways of thinking. The skills and knowledge you acquire as you prepare for your RUAE examination paper will continue to be useful throughout your life.

RUAE key data

Text type	Non-fiction
Length of text	Approximately 1,000 words
Time to complete	1 hour (or possibly more, depending on your individual assessment arrangements)
Number of questions	Approximately nine
Number of marks available	30 marks
Percentage of the total marks available for National 5 English	30%

Reading for Understanding, Analysis and Evaluation: How to do it

To prepare you before you work through the three example question papers for RUAE later in the book, you should work through the following set of straightforward explanations and exercises. These explanations show you how to do each of the different types of questions you are most likely to come across in the RUAE question paper.

The explanations are detailed – study them carefully.

Later, when you are working through the example question papers, you can look to see how the model answers exemplify the advice given in this section of the book.

1 'Using your own words' questions

These questions test your understanding of specific parts of the passage. They ask you to explain a word, a phrase or an idea from the passage using your own words – to prove that you have understood it correctly.

Typically, the question will be worded along the lines of: 'Using your own words as far as possible, explain …' or 'Using your own words as far as possible, summarise …'. The question will often focus on the writer's stance or attitude to the topic they are writing about.

How do I do it? (1)

Consider the following short text and the example questions that follow. The writer is reflecting on changes in social media content and use.

1 There was a time not too long ago when social media felt energising, positive and fun. I loved scrolling through comical, joyful or entertaining images of what my friends and family were up to. I could celebrate the happiness and successes of those close to me with a
5 simple like or a love heart. And, if I shared something affirmative about myself, my friends and family could communicate their instant, real-time positivity back to me. Lately, however, it has all become just so much less authentic. Negativity leaches from insidious algorithms, and manipulative commercial content squeezes out those
10 sweet personal posts that brought me to social media in the first place. It's little wonder that Gen Z are turning increasingly to digital minimalism, curating their feeds and deliberately unfollowing the toxic accounts that have been subconsciously causing them stress. Happily, more teenagers are choosing to take more time off the grid.
15 They want to build more positivity into their lives, through exercise, accessing the natural world and real-life linking up.

Using your own words as far as possible, explain how the writer used to feel about social media. (2 marks)

So, to answer the question above, you will need to do the following:

1. Focus closely on the relevant section of the text and decide what the writer's past feelings were. Re-read the relevant section quickly.

2. Make up your mind about what the writer's attitude is.

3. Select the individual words or phrases that have helped you identify the writer's attitude.

4. Change these words or phrases into new, alternative words or phrases of your own, to show that you have understood correctly.

5. Finally, write your answer using these new words or phrases of your own.

Build your skills (1)

The following table will guide you through the process. Copy and complete the table, then compare your answers to the completed table in *Consolidate your learning*.

Re-read the relevant section.	
Briefly identify the writer's past attitude to social media.	
Note individual words or phrases that helped you to arrive at the conclusion above.	
Paraphrase or reword the writer's words. (You may wish to use a dictionary or thesaurus for this part.)	
Form an answer using a) the writer's attitude as identified by you, and b) your paraphrase/rewording of the writer's words.	

Consolidate your learning (1)

Re-read the relevant section.	Yes
Briefly identify the writer's past attitude to social media.	They liked it very much.
Note individual words or phrases that helped you to arrive at the conclusion above.	'energising', 'positive', 'fun', 'joyful', 'entertaining', 'happiness', 'affirmative'
Paraphrase or reword the writer's words.	invigorating, upbeat, enjoyable, lighthearted, engaging, sense of contentment.
Form an answer using a) the writer's attitude as identified by you, and b) your paraphrase/rewording of the writer's words.	'The writer used to like social media very much. They found it invigorating and enjoyable, and it gave them a sense of contentment.'

So, an answer written out in full might look something like this:

In the past, the writer liked using social media very much (1 mark). *They found it invigorating and enjoyable* (1 mark). *It gave them a sense of contentment* (1 mark).

(The second and third comments above are each sufficient to earn one mark but note a maximum of two marks are available here.)

A concise, bullet-point style answer could save you precious exam time, and might look like this:

- *They liked it a lot* (1 mark)
- *They found it invigorating and enjoyable* (1 mark)
- *It made them feel contented* (1 mark)

(Again, the second and third bullet points are sufficient to earn a mark each, but there are only two marks available here.)

How do I do it? (2)

Now consider the following similar question:

1　Lately, however, it has all become just so much less authentic. Negativity leaches from insidious algorithms, and manipulative commercial content squeezes out those sweet personal posts that brought me to social media in the first place. It's little wonder that
5　Gen Z are turning increasingly to digital minimalism, curating their feeds and deliberately unfollowing the toxic accounts that have been subconsciously causing them stress. Happily, more teenagers are choosing to take more time off the grid. They want to build more positivity into their lives, through exercise, accessing the natural
10　world and real-life linking up.

Look at lines 1 to 7.
Using your own words as far as possible, summarise the writer's more recent feelings about social media. (4 marks)

The process of answering this question is similar to the previous one but note there are more marks available this time round.

1.　Focus closely on the relevant section of the text and decide what the writer's feelings are. Re-read the relevant section quickly.

2.　Make up your mind about what the writer's feelings are.

3.　Select the individual words or phrases that have helped you identify the writer's changed attitude.

4.　Then, again, change these words or phrases into new words or phrases of your own, to show that you have understood correctly. This time, you should aim to cover four different examples – one for each mark available.

5.　Finally, write your answer using these new words or phrases of your own.

Build your skills (2)

Now develop your own answer by copying and completing the following table. Keep the *Consolidate your learning (2)* table below covered while you do this. When you have completed it, you can again compare your answers to those in the completed table in *Consolidate your learning*.

Re-read the relevant section.	
Briefly identify the writer's current attitude to social media.	
Note individual words or phrases that helped you to arrive at the conclusion above.	
Paraphrase or reword the writer's words (minimum of four examples; use a dictionary or thesaurus if you want to).	
Form an answer using a) the writer's attitude as identified by you, and b) your paraphrase/rewording of the writer's words.	

Consolidate your learning (2)

Re-read the relevant section.	Yes
Briefly identify the writer's current attitude to social media.	The writer has a much more negative attitude now.
Note individual words or phrases that helped you to arrive at the conclusion above.	'negativity', 'insidious', 'manipulative', 'toxic', 'causing them stress'
Paraphrase or reword the writer's words (minimum of four examples).	not positive, subtly harmful, coercive, emotionally poisonous, distressing
Form an answer using a) the writer's attitude as identified by you, and b) your paraphrase/rewording of the writer's words.	'The writer's attitude has become much more negative. They now describe social media as lacking positivity, being subtly harmful, coercive, emotionally poisonous and distressing.'

TOP TIP

Vocabulary

The wider your vocabulary is, the better you are likely to do in these questions. Use a dictionary regularly and begin thinking carefully about how you might re-phrase text you have been reading or listening to.

It is recommended that you use bullet points when answering questions which ask you to summarise. Using bullet points will help you to narrow down your answer to the key points required, and will help to prevent you from writing too much, or taking too long on the question. So, a bullet-point style answer to the question on page 11 might look something like this:

- *Attitude has become negative* (1 mark)
- *Social media lacks positive content* (1 mark)
- *Social media harms subtly* (1 mark)
- *Social media can be coercive* (1 mark) or
- *Social media can be harmful to our emotions and mental health* (1 mark)

Again, there are four marks available, so the bullet-pointed answer is slightly longer and more developed than would be needed to reach four marks, but it will give you an idea of the range of answers you could use.

How well you do in these 'using your own words' questions will depend on your understanding and – critically – on your vocabulary, because you must make the best attempt you can to use different words from the original words the writer has used.

Work hard with all your reading and listening – both in English and in other subjects – to develop the range of your vocabulary. The more widely you read, the easier this type of question will become for you.

Find out the meanings of new or unfamiliar words and do your best to remember them.

Candidate question

How many times on average do I need to see a new word before I will be able to remember it?

A Some studies say we need to see a new word between **six** and **ten** times to be sure of learning it. The best advice is to keep reading and listening widely and actively, and to be alert to new or unfamiliar words as you come across them – this will help you to build your vocabulary.

The 'using your own words' questions ask you to find a different way to say the same thing the writer has said. Study the model answers later in the book to see how they rephrase (or paraphrase) the original text in slightly simpler language, often using synonyms.

Looking ahead

Question 1 in the second example question paper on page 51, *Get Myself Connected*, asks you to use your own words to explain the impression the writer creates of the city of Glasgow in this first paragraph of the passage:

> A bitter, wet January wind blows in off the river Clyde. It swirls heavy rain through the illustrious city centre streets and across the doorways of the various historic pubs, theatres and concert halls that serve as the venues for Glasgow's annual *Celtic Connections* traditional music festival.

The question is as follows, and is worth two marks:

Q **Using your own words** as far as possible, explain what impression the writer creates of the city of Glasgow.
You should make two key points in your answer. **(2 marks)**

The following table will help you to understand the process of answering the question.

Original words	Paraphrase ('using own words')	Overall impression
'bitter, wet January wind'	very cold blustery weather, carrying rain	wild and wintry
'heavy rain'	very wet weather	uncomfortable and unpleasant
'illustrious ... streets'	famous, grand streets and architecture	beautiful and uplifting to look at
'historic pubs, theatres and concert halls'	venues with a long history and a great past	a real sense of a glorious past

KEY CONCEPTS

Paraphrase simply means to rephrase using different words, literally to 'tell in other words'.

Candidate question

Will I lose marks if I just can't think of any alternative for a particular word?

 You must do the best you can to change the writer's original words without altering their meaning too much. It is best to replace each word if you can. But if there is one word within a phrase that you just can't think how to paraphrase, try leaving it in your answer, changing the words or phrase around it. You may still be rewarded for making an effort to paraphrase.

You will probably have noticed how the impression of the city divides into two parts: we are given a negative impression of the weather, but a positive impression of the streets, the buildings and the architecture. Your answer should rephrase some of the detail about the bad weather. You could say, for instance, that Glasgow seems 'wintry', 'wild' or 'unpleasant' outdoors. If you are reading very carefully, you will also have noticed the positive words such as 'illustrious' or 'historic'. You might choose similar, related words, and go on to say something like 'the writer gives the impression that Glasgow is a grand and impressive city with an important past'.

Checklist for your answers on 'using your own words':

1. Re-read relevant section.

2. Briefly identify the writer's attitude or stance towards the topic or sub-topic.

3. Highlight or make a mental note of the words that help you to identify the writer's stance.

4. Paraphrase the writer's words.

5. Form your answer with a) the writer's attitude or stance and b) your paraphrase of the writer's words.

Model answers referring to 'using your own words' for your reference:
- *Just Grow Up!*, questions 1, 4, 6, 8, 9 and 10
- *Get Myself Connected*, questions 1, 2, 7 and 9
- *Egg Terrorists*, questions 1, 3, 4, 5, 6 and 9.

2 | 'Examples of language' questions – word choice

You will come across questions which ask you to refer to 'examples of language'. These questions can be answered by referring to a range of different features of language. The 'examples of language' questions are often open, and, once you have learned how to approach them, they are reasonably straightforward to answer. You should also note, however, that some questions which ask about 'examples of language' will specify particular examples of language, such as word choice or sentence structure.

One way to answer questions which ask you to refer to 'examples of language' is by focusing on the writer's choice of specific, individual words. When you are writing about or **analysing** the writer's choice of words, you can home in on specific, interesting, stand-out words, and the effect these particular words have on you as a reader.

How do I do it?

When you are focusing on word choice, you should aim to refer to single, individual words. The shorter the quotation you use in this kind of question, the better. Try not to use more than two words in your quotation. A single word quotation is most effective when you are writing about the writer's word choice.

Look for the words that stand out for some reason – words which may be slightly unusual, or seem to you to be powerful for some reason. Choose the most interesting word(s) from the specified section of text, quote it and provide your own comment on the word.

Generally, you should quote and comment on at least one word per two marks you are looking to pick up in the question (remembering that you might also be expected to look at other examples of language, if the question has asked you to discuss more than one example). Marking instructions tend to suggest one mark for a relevant reference or quote (1) and one mark for a valid comment (1).

Discuss what the connotations (associated meanings) of the word are. Why has the author chosen this particular word? What are the specific, subtle meanings of this word? What does the word **suggest** or what does the word **imply**? Or does the word have any special sound qualities that you might comment on, such as soft, sibilant 's' or 'c' sounds, harsh consonants like 'k', or forceful plosives such as 'p' or 'b' sounds?

A useful approach is to quote the word, then lead into your comment by saying 'suggests ...' or 'implies ...' or 'makes me think that ...'. The quality of the comment you add after 'suggests' or 'implies' will earn you your marks.

Consider the following short text and the question that follows. The writer has been observing seal pups in Shetland and reflects on the challenges they face.

TOP TIP

Questions on language will ask you how the writer uses language to create a particular impression of the subject. When focusing on word choice, as you choose which words to analyse and comment on, think about the impression the writer is trying to create. Choose words to comment on which are slightly unusual or different – words which stand out.

1 The thousands of baby seals which ornament the narrow, rocky inlets
or *geos* of the Shetland coast in late autumn really are the last word
in aquatic mammal cute. Adorable fluffy off-white balls of milky
blubber with soulful, lustrous eyes, they are entirely dependent on
5 their mothers in the days immediately following birth. After three
weeks or so, when their creamy white baby fur – known as *lanugo* –
begins to give way to the mottled young adult coat, the seals become
granite boulders lying among the wavering seaweed strands and the
crashing sea swells which thunder into the *geo*. It is shortly after this
10 that they must be weaned from their mothers' milk and begin to
hunt fish for themselves, running the gauntlet of the predatory killer
whales that sweep like submarines through the deeper waters at the
mouth of the inlet.

Q Look at lines 1 to 4.

By referring to **two** examples of language (word choice), explain how the
writer makes it clear that they find the seal pups appealing. (4 marks)

So, to answer this question, you will have to do the following things:

1. Quickly re-read the relevant section.
2. Home in on positive words that contribute to the idea of the seal
   pups being 'appealing'.
3. Because there are four marks available, choose two different words
   or short phrases which contribute to this idea.
4. For your answer, quote each word, followed by your developed
   comment on the qualities of the word and how it conveys the
   positive 'appeal' of the seal pups.

Build your skills

Develop your own answer by copying and completing the following
table. Once you have finished the task, you can compare your answers
with the completed table in *Consolidate your learning*.

Re-read the relevant section.	
Focus on stand-out words that convey 'appeal'.	
Select the two most promising examples.	
Quote each in turn, followed by your own developed comment on the qualities of the word. You may wish to begin this part by using the word 'suggests', 'conveys' or 'implies'.	

Consolidate your learning

Re-read the relevant section.	Yes
Focus on stand-out words that convey 'appeal'.	'ornament', 'adorable', 'soulful', 'lustrous'
Select the two most promising examples.	'ornament' and 'lustrous'
Quote each in turn, followed by your own developed comment on the qualities of the word.	'Ornament', used here as a verb, suggests the seal pups are appealing objects of beauty and interest. 'Lustrous' implies their eyes are shining beautifully with reflected light, that their eyes have an attractive glazed appearance.

So, an example answer to the question on page 16 written out in full might look something like this:

'Ornament' (1 mark)*, used unusually here as a verb, suggests the pups are appealing, interesting, beautiful objects that enhance their surroundings* (1 mark).

'Lustrous' (1 mark) *suggests the eyes shine with beautiful light, that they have a glazed appearance, that the eyes are attractive* (1 mark).

Alternatively, a concise, bullet-point answer might look like this:

* *'Ornament'* (1 mark) *– implies beauty, decoration, enhanced surroundings* (1 mark)
* *'Lustrous'* (1 mark) *– suggests a glazed look, shining, attractive* (1 mark)

Looking ahead

Question 8 from the third example question paper on page 59, *Egg Terrorists*, is about how the writer uses 'examples of language' to convey their opinion of the people who work to protect wild birds and their eggs. You could focus on word choice for your answer to this question. The question is as follows:

Q **By referring to two examples of language, explain how the writer makes clear their view of those who work to protect the birds. (4 marks)**

The question asks you to consider the following extract:

But there is also a growing band of determined individuals who give their time and energy to combat the egg thieves. In the 1950s, when rare ospreys returned to nest in Scotland for the first time in nearly forty years, a small group of hardy amateur birdwatchers worked months of gruelling shifts to guard the first vulnerable nests from egg thieves. Their story has become part of conservation legend.

Focusing just on word choice for now, try it yourself by copying and completing the following table.

Quote writer's original word/ 'stand-out' word	Add your comment – what does the word suggest to you? What does the word make you think of? Connotations? Tone? Sounds?	What impression is given?
'legend'	strong positive, implies memorable story, frequent re-telling, heroic	gives impression of heroism and respect, a powerful story that will be told throughout generations

It might seem obvious to you that the writer's view of these people is very positive. But how exactly do the individual words contribute to this positive impression? Which particular words stand out, and what could you say about them? You might pick out 'combat', 'gruelling' or 'legend'. You need to include at least one worthwhile point per word to earn your marks. So, for your answer, you could write something like:

The writer creates a very strong positive impression of the people who helped the birds. They use words like 'combat', which has connotations of fighting and danger, 'gruelling', which implies that conditions were very tough, and 'legend', which suggests what they did was so important it became a kind of special story that was remembered for many, many years. These words used together create the impression that the writer admires the conservationists very much.

Model answers referring to word choice (or more general 'examples of language') for your reference:
- *Just Grow Up!*, questions 2, 3, 5 and 7
- *Get Myself Connected*, questions 3, 4, 6 and 8
- *Egg Terrorists*, questions 2, 7 and 8.

Checklist for your answers on 'word choice':

1. Select and quote 'stand-out' word(s).

2. Lead into your comment, for example using 'implies', 'suggests' or 'makes me think'.

3. Make your comment, linking back to the impression or idea from the question.

4. Check you've covered enough individual words for the marks available. For each two marks available, you should quote one word (1) and provide one detailed comment (1).

You may well have already done some work on imagery – especially similes and metaphors – in primary school or in the early stages of secondary school. You will be looking for the images or comparisons the writer has created and commenting on the effects of these images.

You will almost certainly want to write about imagery to answer questions that invite you to discuss 'examples of language'. The first thing you should do is 'explain the image'. This simply requires you to identify the actual, real thing that the writer is describing, and then say what it is that the writer is comparing this 'real' thing to (explain the invented simile or metaphor).

Some teachers like to refer to the real subject as the 'literal root' of the image and refer to the invented part (the created simile or metaphor) as the 'figurative extension' of the image. You can use these terms if you find they help you. The exercises that follow will guide you through the process.

KEY CONCEPTS

The first thing to remember when starting to think about **imagery** is that the term 'imagery' includes similes (comparisons using 'like' or 'as'), metaphors (direct comparisons where one thing is said to be another) and personifications (a specific type of metaphor where something that is not alive is compared to a human being).

How do I do it?

Consider again the short passage about the baby seals:

> 1   The thousands of baby seals which ornament the narrow, rocky inlets or *geos* of the Shetland coast in late autumn really are the last word in aquatic mammal cute. Adorable fluffy off-white balls of milky blubber with soulful, lustrous eyes, they are entirely dependent on
> 5   their mothers in the days immediately following birth. After three weeks or so, when their creamy white baby fur – known as *lanugo* – begins to give way to the mottled young adult coat, **the seals become granite boulders** lying among the wavering seaweed strands and the crashing sea swells which thunder into the *geo*. It is shortly after
> 10   this that they must be weaned from their mothers' milk and begin to hunt fish for themselves, running the gauntlet of the predatory **killer whales that sweep like submarines** through the deeper waters at the mouth of the inlet.

Reading very carefully, you may notice that the writer has used two comparisons, or 'images', in this passage. The images have been set in bold to help you. One image is used to describe the seals, and another is used to describe the killer whales. The comparison used to describe the seals is a metaphor – a direct comparison where they are said to be something else, something that they are not really. Don't be confused when the writer says, 'the seals become granite boulders'. They don't really (or 'literally') become boulders. The writer is choosing to compare the seals to granite boulders to help us imagine what they are like.

Likewise, towards the end of the extract, the writer compares the killer whales to 'submarines'. This 'image' may be a little easier for you to spot because it is a simile and uses the word 'like'.

So, what kind of questions might we expect to see focusing on imagery? These would be either questions asking us broadly to consider 'examples of language' or questions that ask us directly to write about 'imagery'. Sometimes, questions will ask generally about 'examples of language' and then specify 'imagery' as one of the features you are required to comment on.

So, to answer this type of question, you will need to do the following things:

1. Quickly and accurately re-read the relevant lines.
2. Locate the image (simile can be confirmed if you see the word 'like' or 'as'; metaphor is a direct comparison).
3. In your mind, be clear about what is being described (the 'literal root' of the image) and what it is being compared to (the 'figurative extension' of the image).
4. Tease out or 'unpack' the similarities between the literal root and the figurative extension. This will help you to understand what impression the writer is aiming to create.
5. Write your answer, making clear you have located the images, understood the literal and figurative parts of the image, and can make some connections between the two.

Build your skills (1)

Here is a simplified question focused on one image from the passage above:

> **Q** By referring to **one** example of language (imagery), explain how the writer makes it clear that the baby seals have gone through physical changes. (2 marks)

Develop your own answer by copying and completing the following table. Once you have finished the task, you can compare your answers with the completed table in *Consolidate your learning*.

Quickly and accurately re-read the relevant lines.	
Locate the image.	
Be clear about literal root and figurative extension.	
'Unpack' similarities, make connections, identify the impression(s) the writer creates.	
Write an answer which quotes and unpacks the image and identifies the impression(s) the writer has created.	

Consolidate your learning (1)

Quickly and accurately re-read the relevant lines.	Yes
Locate the image.	'seals become granite boulders'
Be clear about literal root and figurative extension.	literal root – seal pups figurative extension – granite boulders
'Unpack' similarities, make connections, identify the impression(s) the writer creates.	large, rounded, heavy, smooth, solid, mottled or spotted black-and-white colouring
Write an answer which quotes and unpacks the image and identifies the impression(s) the writer has created.	The metaphor comparing the seals to 'granite boulders' suggests they have become larger and heavier, and that their bodies are smooth and rounded. It also makes me think their colour has changed from off-white to a more patchy black and white.

So, a developed answer to the question on page 20, written in full, might look something like this:

The metaphor comparing the seals to 'granite boulders' (1 mark) *implies they have become larger and heavier, and that their bodies may be smooth and rounded* (1 mark). *It also suggests to me that their colour has changed from off-white to a patchier black and white* (1 mark).

A concise, bullet-point answer to the same question might look something like this:

- *Metaphor – 'granite boulders'* (1 mark) *implies roundness, large size and weight* (1 mark)
- *Also implies change from off-white to patchy black-and-white colour* (1 mark)

Again, note that while the answers on page 20 show a range of responses and where marks could be earned, there are a maximum of two marks available for this question.

KEY CONCEPTS

A **metaphor** is a direct comparison where one thing is said to be another thing. The word metaphor comes from ancient Greek and means 'carrying from one place to another'.

Build your skills (2)

Here is a second, simplified question focused on another image from the passage above:

Q By referring to **one** example of language (imagery), explain the impression the writer creates of the killer whales. **(2 marks)**

Develop your own answer by copying and completing the following table. Keep the *Consolidate your learning (2)* table below covered while you do this. Once you have finished the task, you can compare your answers with the completed table in *Consolidate your learning (2)*.

Quickly and accurately re-read the relevant lines.	
Locate the image.	
Be clear about literal root and figurative extension.	
'Unpack' similarities, make connections, identify the impression(s) the writer creates.	
Write an answer which quotes and unpacks the image and identifies the impression(s) the writer has created.	

Consolidate your learning (2)

Quickly and accurately re-read the relevant lines.	Yes
Locate the image.	'killer whales that sweep like submarines'
Be clear about literal root and figurative extension.	literal root – killer whales figurative extension – submarines
'Unpack' similarities, make connections, identify the impression(s) the writer creates.	Simile suggests large, fast-moving, elongated, dark, dangerous, mysterious, sinister, predatory underwater shapes.
Write an answer which quotes and unpacks the image and identifies the impression(s) the writer has created.	The simile comparing the killer whales to 'submarines' suggests they are large, swift, elongated, dark, moving objects with a sinister, predatory purpose.

So, a developed answer to the question, written in full, might look something like this:

The simile comparing the killer whales to 'submarines' (1 mark) *suggests they are large, swift, elongated, dark, moving objects with a sinister, predatory purpose* (1 mark).

A concise, bullet-point answer to the same question might look something like this:

- *Simile – 'like submarines'* (1 mark) *implies intimidating size and speed* (1 mark), or
- *Implies elongated shape, dark colour, dangerous purpose* (1 mark)

Again, note that while the answers above show a range of responses and where marks could be earned, there are a maximum of two marks available for this question.

Looking ahead

Later in this book, question 3 from the first example question paper on page 44, *Just Grow Up!*, invites you to refer to an 'example of language'. There are two parts to this question. First, you may wish to focus on the image 'like an overheated engine running on its own burning oil'. The 'literal root' of this image is Andy Murray himself, and the 'figurative extension' of the image is the overheating engine.

The question is as follows:

> **Q** **By referring to one example of language, show how the writer creates the impression that Andy Murray had lost control. (2 marks)**

In the second part of your answer, you should analyse the effect of the image. Although this may sound a little complicated, remember that all you really have to do is think about what the figurative part of the image suggests to you about the literal root. You are being asked to say how the invented simile or metaphor adds to your understanding of the real person or thing being described.

So, in the question about the image of the 'overheated engine', we might say that the image suggests the player is out of control, in danger, angry or even aggressive.

As with the word choice questions, it is a good idea to begin the second part of your answer with the word 'suggests' or 'implies'. If you can think of and write down two or three connections between the literal root of the image and the figurative extension, then you will do well in these questions.

TOP TIP

You really do need to 'unpack' the image the writer has created. Try to think of as many reasonable connections as you can between the person, object or thing being described (the **literal root**) and the simile or metaphor that the writer has created (the figurative extension).

Model answers referring to imagery for your reference:
- *Just Grow Up!*, questions 3 and 5
- *Get Myself Connected*, questions 4, 6 and 8
- *Egg Terrorists*, questions 2, 7 and 8.

Candidate question

Can you give an example of a 'personification', the special kind of image/metaphor that was mentioned earlier?

A Yes, of course. A personification is where something which is not alive is presented as if it is a human being, hence the word 'person' in the name. For example, 'the cruel North wind blew his icy breath across the frozen loch' or 'benevolent nature has her own ways of providing for us'. Language also contains what are known as 'dead' metaphors, which have become so common in everyday use that we hardly notice them, for example 'the **leg** of the table' or 'the **eye** of the storm'.

4   'Examples of language' questions – sentence structure

Many people find thinking about 'sentence structure' in the RUAE paper challenging. Often, people are not sure which features to look for to describe sentence structure. Once you have learned about a few of the features writers use when they are constructing their sentences, you will find writing about sentence structure relatively straightforward.

How do I do it?

'Sentence structure' means the way that the sentences have been put together, shaped or 'structured' by the writer. You may refer to individual sentences or you may look at more than one sentence from the specified section of the text. You might choose to compare different sentences within the specified section of text. You may choose to pick out or identify features of sentence structure from an individual sentence. As with analysis of word choice or imagery, you should then discuss how these features affect you as a reader.

Candidate question

Is writing about sentence structure the hardest part of RUAE?

A Writing about sentence structure can be challenging. But if you study this section of the book carefully you will build up the range of comments you are able to make about sentence structure, and you will master it. Being able to analyse and write about the shapes and structures of sentences can potentially gain you marks.

Here is a list of ten key features of sentence structure that you can refer to when answering RUAE questions. If you study this list carefully and memorise the features, you will have more than enough to write about on sentence structure when you are looking for 'examples of language'.

1 **Short sentences.** Think about the lengths of the sentences. If the sentence is particularly short and simple, you might describe it as being 'forceful', 'abrupt', 'powerful' or even 'punchy'.

2 **Long sentences.** If the sentence is particularly long, it may be that it adds or lists details to create power or builds up towards a climax. Sometimes a long sentence seems to be building to a climax but ends up with a deliberate and disappointing **anticlimax**. A long sentence can be described as having a 'cumulative effect' if it creates a build-up.

3 **Listing.** Many sentences contain lists. It is not enough just to say the sentence contains a list, but you can earn marks if you say that a list 'creates the impression' of something. For instance, 'the list creates the impression of boredom', or 'the list convinces us that there are many different reasons', or 'the list gives the impression of great variety'.

4 **Statement, question or command.** All sentences belong to one of the following three categories: statements, questions and commands. Statements are the commonest in writing, while questions or commands are less common and are often worth commenting on. A 'rhetorical question' is a question that is used simply to arouse our interest, to invite us to agree with a point or to persuade us. The title of the first example passage in this book – *Just Grow Up!* – is a command and sounds very forceful and emphatic. The passage *Egg Terrorists* begins with a question. This is quite unusual, and draws us in to the topic of text: 'What exactly is it about the eggs of wild birds that fascinates and captivates us?'

5 **Syntax/word order.** Is the order of the words in any way unusual? Sometimes writers will deliberately play around with the normal 'syntax' (the arrangement of words in a sentence) to emphasise particular words. So, for instance, the unusual syntax of a phrase like 'And cold it was' places more emphasis on the word 'cold' than the more usual 'And it was cold'.

KEY CONCEPTS

A **rhetorical question** is a question that is used to draw our attention to something, or to emphasise something, rather than genuinely seeking an answer.

6 **A little bit of grammar – minor sentences.** Some very basic knowledge of grammar can help you, too. To be grammatically typical, a sentence should contain a subject or noun and a verb. If a sentence is lacking a subject or a verb, it is called a 'non-sentence' or a 'minor sentence'. Minor sentences look slightly odd, and are sometimes used by writers to create emphasis, such as in paragraph six of the passage *Egg Terrorists*, where the writer includes the minor sentence 'And rightly so.' This short minor sentence creates a sense of firm agreement.

7 **A little bit more grammar – clauses.** A part of a sentence containing a verb is called a 'clause'. If a sentence has just one verb/clause, it is called a 'simple sentence'. If a sentence has more than one clause and the clauses are joined by a conjunction or conjunctions, such as 'and', 'but' or 'then', the sentence is described as a 'compound sentence'. If the sentence has a clause separated from the main clause by a comma or commas, the sentence is described as a 'complex sentence'. You may choose to use these terms as you discuss the structures of sentences, and the effects of these structures.

Candidate question

Do I need to spend time learning about grammar such as clauses and minor sentences for RUAE?

A A little knowledge about simpler sentence structure concepts such as sentence length, punctuation, listing or rhetorical questions will stand you in good stead. Studying the slightly more challenging materials here on concepts such as clauses and minor sentences may help you to increase your overall mark.

8 **Contrasting or different sentences.** Look out for contrasting types of sentences within paragraphs. Writers sometimes alternate simple and complex sentences, or short and long sentences, for effect. For instance, a short or simple sentence can really stand out if it is placed at the end of a paragraph made up of long or complex sentences.

9 **Punctuation.** Don't forget that you may also write about punctuation when you are considering sentence structures or 'examples of language'. For example, the colon (:) and the semicolon (;) are two very important punctuation marks. Knowing what they are for and how they work can really help you to analyse the structure of a sentence.

The colon (:) is used to introduce an expansion, an explanation or the definition of an idea that comes before it in the first part of the sentence. The colon can also be used to introduce a list (in this case the list provides the expansion, explanation or definition). The colon is sometimes used to introduce a sense of drama in a sentence and can create a sort of 'pregnant' pause.

The semicolon (;) can be used instead of a full stop between two sentences, if the sentences are very closely related. The semicolon helps the reader to understand that the two sentences belong together in the text, almost as one unit. The semicolon can also be used to separate items in a list, if the items are groups of words, rather than individual words.

The following extract from the passage *Just Grow Up!* shows a colon being used to introduce an expansion on the idea of Andy Murray's perceived 'lack of grace', and semicolons being used to separate the three items in the list:

> His lack of grace became a talking point: he was all testosterone and no charisma; he hogged the PlayStation and guzzled junk food; he was unapologetically dour in press conferences.

10 **The 'power of three'.** Finally, if you are instructed to write about aspects of sentence structure, remember the power of three. Three-part lists or structures in sentences or paragraphs provide a very effective way of persuading the reader or emphasising a point the writer wants to make. Think about the extract from the *Just Grow Up!* passage again:

> His lack of grace became a talking point: he was all testosterone and no charisma; he hogged the PlayStation and guzzled junk food; he was unapologetically dour in press conferences.

If a writer is trying to persuade us of something, the first example will get our attention, the second will begin to persuade us and the third will probably convince us. Three-part structures are a well-known feature of rhetoric (the ancient art of using language to persuade readers or listeners). Just as you might refer to a 'rhetorical question', so too can you refer to a 'three-part rhetorical structure', if you are discussing the way the writer has used sentence structure.

Now consider the following short text. In this text, the writer is reflecting on the linked issues of climate change and global poverty.

> 1   There is now very little doubt in the minds of rational people that climate change is a real and grave concern. Coral reefs are bleaching. Deserts are expanding. Forests are burning. Our profligate, consumerist culture, our selfish, privileged greed and our mindless
> 5   egotistical desires are killing the planet we live on and the creatures we share it with. And yet, this most profound problem of our age is closely linked to the other extreme challenge facing millions across the globe: the problem of abject, soul-crushing poverty. How can the estimated 10% of the world's population who are living in extreme
> 10   poverty be expected to consider the environment? People existing on three dollars' income a day or less literally can't afford to be worrying about microplastics, carbon emissions or shrinking glaciers. And the world's poor are those who will bear the brunt of the apocalyptic future effects of climate change, while the rich will be relatively
> 15   insulated from these effects. Something must be done.

Reading very carefully, you should consider whether you can spot any of the features of sentence structure covered in the previous section within the relevant lines. You might want to start by considering the different lengths of sentences, and then home in on any specific features you can identify.

These step-by-step instructions should help you at this stage:

1. Quickly and accurately re-read the relevant lines.
2. Look for any sentences which seem long or short. Are the sentences questions, statements or commands? Can you spot any patterns or specific features?
3. In your mind, be clear about the writer's point of view towards the subject. (In this case, it is probably quite obvious that the writer views the subject as a serious problem.)
4. Choose a minimum of two references or features of sentence structure and consider how these features contribute to the sense of seriousness.
5. Write your answer, identifying at least two features and making clear how they contribute to the sense of seriousness.

Build your skills (1)

Now consider the following question, which refers back to the short passage on climate change and poverty.

> 1 There is now very little doubt in the minds of rational people that climate change is a real and grave concern. Coral reefs are bleaching. Deserts are expanding. Forests are burning. Our profligate, consumerist culture, our selfish, privileged greed, and our mindless
> 5 egotistical desires are killing the planet we live on and the creatures we share it with.

Q Look at lines 1 to 6.

By referring to **two** examples of sentence structure, explain how the writer makes it clear that climate change is a serious problem. (4 marks)

Develop your own answer by copying and completing the following table. Once you have finished the task, you can compare your answers with the completed table in *Consolidate your learning*.

Quickly and accurately re-read the relevant lines.	
Consider lengths and types of sentences. Are there any patterns?	
Be clear about the writer's point of view during the relevant section.	
Select your sentence structure reference(s) and feature(s).	
Prepare your answer by selecting your examples of features, describing their effect and linking to the writer's point of view. One feature (1) plus one comment (1) for each pair of marks available.	

Quickly and accurately re-read the relevant lines.	Yes
Consider lengths and types of sentences. Are there any patterns?	Sentence one ('There is now very little ...') is a statement. The next three sentences ('Coral reefs ...' etc.) are all short, simple statements and follow the same pattern. Sentence five ('Our profligate ...') is long and complex.
Be clear about the writer's point of view during the relevant section.	Views the situation seriously. There is even a sense of anger.
Select your sentence structure reference(s) and feature(s).	'Coral reefs are bleaching. Deserts are expanding. Forests are burning.' Three simple sentences follow the same pattern, create a forceful list and emphasise the seriousness. The sentence beginning 'Our profligate ...' is long and complex, building up through clauses to a climax 'killing the planet ... and the creatures we share it with.'
Prepare your answer by selecting your examples of features, describing their effect and linking to the writer's point of view. One feature (1) plus one comment (1) for each pair of marks available.	The writer uses three short, simple sentences – 'Coral reefs are bleaching.' etc. – creating a forceful list of serious environmental problems. The sentence beginning 'Our profligate, consumerist culture ...' is long and complex, building up another list of things we are doing wrong, before reaching a climax with 'killing the planet ... and the creatures we share it with.' This again emphasises the seriousness of the situation.

So, a developed answer written in full might look something like this:

The writer uses three short, simple statements – 'Coral reefs are bleaching.' etc. (1 mark) – creating a forceful list of serious environmental problems (1 mark).

The sentence beginning 'Our profligate, consumerist culture ...' (1 mark) is long and complex, building up another list of things we are doing wrong, before reaching a climax with 'killing the planet ... and the creatures we share it with.' (1 mark) This again emphasises the seriousness of the situation.

A concise, bullet-point answer might look something like this:

* *'Coral reefs are bleaching ... Forests are burning.' (1 mark) – short forceful listing creates serious impression (1 mark)*
* *Sentence beginning 'Our profligate, consumerist culture ...' (1 mark) is long and complex, builds list and reaches powerful climax at 'killing the planet', emphasising seriousness (1 mark)*

I'm learning a lot about language as I prepare for RUAE. Is it OK for me to use some of the techniques I'm learning about here in my own writing, either for the National 5 critical essay or my portfolio piece?

A Absolutely! This is how we learn best, and if you can employ any of these techniques in your own writing this will have the double benefit of helping you to remember them **and** enhancing your own writing.

Build your skills (2)

Now consider the following question, which refers again to the passage on climate change and poverty.

8   How can the estimated 10% of the world's population who are living in extreme poverty be expected to consider the environment? People existing on three dollars' income a day or less literally can't afford to be worrying about microplastics, carbon emissions or shrinking
12   glaciers. And the world's poor are those who will bear the brunt of the apocalyptic future effects of climate change, while the rich will be relatively insulated from these effects. Something must be done.

Q Look at lines 8 to 14.
By referring to **two** examples of sentence structure, explain how the writer makes it clear that poverty is a serious concern. (4 marks)

Develop your own answer by copying and completing the following table. Once you have finished the task, you can compare your answers with the completed table in *Consolidate your learning*.

Quickly and accurately re-read the relevant lines.	
Consider lengths and types of sentences. Are there any patterns?	
Be clear about the writer's point of view during the relevant section.	
Select your sentence structure reference(s) and feature(s).	
Prepare your answer by selecting your examples of features, describing their effect and linking to the writer's point of view. One feature (1) plus one comment (1) for each pair of marks available.	

Consolidate your learning (2)

Quickly and accurately re-read the relevant lines.	Yes
Consider lengths and types of sentences. Are there any patterns?	First sentence is a rhetorical question. Second sentence uses a three-part list for emphasis. Third sentence is balanced with reference to the poor and the rich. Final sentence is particularly short and direct.
Be clear about the writer's point of view during the relevant section.	The writer takes poverty very seriously.
Select your sentence structure reference(s) and feature(s).	Rhetorical question in first sentence: 'How can …'. Short, punchy, simple sentence at close of paragraph.
Prepare your answer by selecting your examples of features, describing their effect and linking to the writer's point of view. One feature (1) plus one comment (1) for each pair of marks available.	Rhetorical question ('How can …') (1) draws our attention to serious point about the absurdity of expecting the poor to care about the environment (1). Short, punchy final sentence ('Something must …') (1) contrasts with long sentences and stresses seriousness/call to action (1).

So, a developed answer written in full might look something like this:

The writer uses a rhetorical question ('How can …') (1 mark) to draw our attention to the serious point about the absurdity of expecting the poor to care about the environment (1 mark). A short, punchy final sentence ('Something must be done.') (1 mark) emphasises the writer's seriousness and is a call to action, urging us to do something about the situation (1 mark).

A concise, bullet-point answer might look something like this:

- *'How can … consider the environment?' – rhetorical question (1 mark) emphasises seriousness and absurdity (1 mark)*
- *'Something must be done.' – short, simple, punchy sentence (1 mark) makes forceful call to readers (1 mark)*

Candidate question

Do I have to include long detailed quotations from the passage in my RUAE answers?

A No, you don't. As long as your quote or reference makes it clear which feature you are referring to, it will be fine. You may have noticed in the examples here that some of the quotes/references are simply placed in brackets within the answer or sometimes a shortened form of the sentence with an ellipsis (…) has been used. This can save you precious exam time.

Looking ahead

Model answers referring to sentence structure (or more general 'examples of language') for your reference:

- *Just Grow Up!*, question 2
- *Get Myself Connected*, questions 3, 4, 6 and 8
- *Egg Terrorists*, questions 2, 7 and 8.

5 | A note on 'examples of language'

It is important for you to remember that 'language' or 'examples of language' are terms you will come across regularly when studying English at National 5 level and beyond. If a question asks you to refer to 'examples of language' or 'how does the writer use language to …', this is a good opportunity for you, because 'examples of language' is actually a very broad phrase that takes in word choice, sentence structure, punctuation, imagery and all of the other features dealt with in this section of the book. You should look closely at the specified part of the text and pick out some of the interesting features. Use a short quote to illustrate, name the example you intend to discuss and make your comment, leading in with the word 'suggests' or 'implies'. Importantly, you should try to show how these examples are used to create a particular impression of the subject in question.

Candidate question

How many examples of language should I cover in my answer?

A This depends on the number of marks available. The question will often tell you how many examples you should cover. Check to make sure you've covered the required number: every two marks means one example of language. You will be awarded one mark for your quote/reference (1) and one mark for your comment/analysis (1).

Checklist for your answers on 'examples of language':

1. Briefly quote the example.

2. Identify the technique or feature used (image, word choice, feature of sentence structure or punctuation).

3. Describe the effect or 'unpack' the feature. What impression is created? What effect does it have on the reader?

Model answers referring to examples of language for your reference:

- *Just Grow Up!*, questions 2, 3, 5 and 7
- *Get Myself Connected*, questions 3, 4, 6 and 8
- *Egg Terrorists*, questions 2, 7 and 8.

Sometimes, if a writer wants to move on from one topic to another, they will include a sentence or a short paragraph that serves as a 'link' between the two different topics or ideas. Typically, this linking sentence or paragraph will include a word or phrase that connects or 'links' back to the previous idea or topic, followed by another word or phrase that identifies or 'links' forward to the idea or topic that the writer intends to discuss next.

How do I do it?

If you are asked a question about how a particular sentence within the RUAE text helps to provide a link, you should first pick out the word or phrase that links back to a previous idea. Quote it and say as clearly as you can what the previous idea is. Alternatively, pick out the word or phrase that links forward to the idea the writer is moving on to, quote it, and say as clearly as you can what the next idea in the passage is.

Study the following list, which will help you to memorise the process:

1. Re-read the relevant sentence, which will be identified in the question.
2. Look back over the text immediately before the sentence. You will probably have to look over multiple sentences or a whole paragraph. Think about the topic of the text immediately before the link sentence. Be clear in your mind what the topic is.
3. Look ahead to the text immediately following the sentence. Again, you will probably have to look over multiple sentences or a whole paragraph. Think about the topic of the text coming after the link sentence. Be clear in your mind what this new topic is.
4. Now look again at the link sentence itself. Pick out the word or phrase that connects back to the previous topic. Then pick out the word or phrase that connects forward to the next topic.
5. Create your answer by identifying and quoting a) the reference from the link sentence that links back, and the previous topic it links back to, **or** b) the reference from the link sentence that links forward, and the new topic it links forward to. You will gain two marks for any correctly identified reference and an accurate description of what it links back or forward to. You can also gain two marks by correctly identifying the precise selections from within the link sentence going in both directions.

Build your skills

Here, we will return to the text about climate change and poverty. Re-read the extract, focusing closely now on the sentence in bold, which provides a link between the writer's ideas at this point in the passage:

1	There is now very little doubt in the minds of rational people that
	climate change is a real and grave concern. Coral reefs are bleaching.
	Deserts are expanding. Forests are burning. Our profligate,
	consumerist culture, our selfish, privileged greed, and our mindless
5	egotistical desires are killing the planet we live on and the creatures
	we share it with. **And yet, this most profound problem of our age**
	is closely linked to the other extreme challenge facing millions
	across the globe: the problem of abject, soul-crushing poverty. How
	can the estimated 10% of the world's population who are living in
10	extreme poverty be expected to consider the environment? People
	existing on three dollars' income a day or less literally can't afford
	to be worrying about microplastics, carbon emissions, or shrinking
	glaciers. And the world's poor are those who will bear the brunt of
	the apocalyptic future effects of climate change, while the rich will be
15	relatively insulated from these effects. Something must be done.

Q By referring to any part of the sentence in lines 6–8 ('And yet … soul-crushing poverty.'), explain how it helps to provide a link between the writer's ideas at this point in the passage. (2 marks)

Develop your own answer by copying and completing the following table. Once you have finished the task, you can compare your answers with the completed table in *Consolidate your learning*.

Re-read the relevant sentence.	
Look back over *previous* text and identify topic.	
Look forward over *following* text and identify topic.	
Look closely at link sentence and identify precise parts linking back and forward.	
Create your answer identifying either a) previous idea and reference linking back, b) forthcoming idea and reference linking forward, or c) reference linking back *and* reference linking forward.	

Consolidate your learning

Re-read the relevant sentence.	Yes
Look back over the *previous* text and identify topic.	Topic is climate change.
Look forward over *following* text and identify topic.	Topic is poverty.
Look closely at link sentence and identify precise parts linking back and forward.	'most profound problem of our age' refers back 'soul-crushing poverty' links forward
Create your answer identifying either a) previous idea and reference linking back, b) forthcoming idea and reference linking forward, or c) reference linking back *and* reference linking forward.	Answer a) 'most profound problem of our age' refers back to the topic of climate change. Answer b) 'soul-crushing poverty' links forward to the topic of poverty. Answer c) 'most profound problem' links back, 'soul crushing poverty' links forward.

So, a range of developed answers written in full would include the following:

The phrase 'most profound problem of our age' (1 mark) *refers back to the topic of climate change* (1 mark).

The phrase 'soul-crushing poverty' (1 mark) *links forward to the topic of a severe lack of resources* (1 mark).

The phrase 'most profound problem' links back (1 mark)*, while the phrase 'soul crushing poverty' links forward* (1 mark).

Concise, bullet-point answers might look something like these:

- *'Profound problem'* (1 mark) *refers back to climate change* (1 mark)
- *'Soul-crushing poverty'* (1 mark) *refers forward to severe lack of money and resources* (1 mark)
- *'Profound problem' links back* (1 mark)*, while 'soul-crushing poverty' links forward* (1 mark)

Looking ahead

Paragraph five of the passage *Get Myself Connected* is an example of a 'linking' paragraph:

> But what many failed to realise about the folk players and singers of the seventies and eighties was that these musicians were vital to the continuation of our rich musical and lyric traditions. They were the few remaining living links to the great music of Scotland's past.

The phrase 'folk players and singers of the seventies and eighties' links back to the previous paragraph, which is about folk music in Scotland during these decades. The phrase 'the great music of Scotland's past' links forward to the topic of the next paragraph, which is the wider history of Scottish music, going further back into the distant past.

Checklist for your answers on 'links':

1. Re-read the relevant sentence.

2. Look back over the previous text and identify topic.

3. Look forward over forthcoming text and identify topic.

4. Look over link sentence and pinpoint parts linking a) back and b) forward.

5. Write answer identifying a) previous idea and reference back or b) forthcoming idea and reference forward or c) reference linking back and reference linking forward.

Model answer referring to links in the text for your reference:
- *Get Myself Connected*, question 5.

7 | Implication

It is useful if you understand the concept of 'implication'. 'To imply' means the same as 'to hint' or 'to suggest'. If a text 'implies' something, it means that an idea is suggested to us, without being stated directly. The writer may use word choice or imagery or other examples of language to suggest an impression of a person or thing, without being explicit about their feelings towards the subject. So, in the passage *Egg Terrorists*, the writer does not actually state that they dislike the egg thieves, but they make their feelings clear through word choice and imagery; it can be said that they 'imply' their negative view. The opposite of 'to imply' is 'to infer'. So, the text (or the writer) implies, while the reader infers; we 'infer' from the text of *Egg Terrorists* that the writer dislikes the egg collectors.

TOP TIP

If you can create a linking sentence or paragraph in a piece of writing of your own, this will improve your writing *and* help you to remember the process for RUAE.

Looking ahead

Model answers referring to the concept of implication for your reference:

- *Just Grow Up!*, question 8
- *Egg Terrorists*, questions 7 and 8.

8 | Questions that ask you to 'summarise'

How do I do it?

One of the skills that may be tested in the RUAE paper is your ability to 'summarise' the main ideas in the text, or in a section of the text. To 'summarise' simply means to pick out the main points and explain them in a shorter way. Questions which ask you to summarise are again assessing your understanding of what you have read, and you will be instructed to 'use your own words' as far as possible.

You are being asked to identify the most important ideas in the text and outline them briefly. To answer this question, you should skim again through the text (or the specified section of the text) and consider which ideas you feel are most important. You may choose to underline or highlight what you consider to be the writer's key ideas. Then, in your answer, you should outline these ideas, using your own words as far as possible.

A summary question might ask you to summarise the main ideas in relation to a specific aspect of the passage, such as in question 10 of the passage *Just Grow Up!* which focuses on the presentation of the media in this text. Alternatively, a summary question may ask you to summarise the main ideas of the passage, or a section of the passage. In either case, you need to re-read quickly and carefully to spot the relevant ideas.

It is important to think about the number of marks available for the summary, as this will give you some idea of how much detail is required, how many main points to include or how many bullet points you should use. Finally, if the question asks you to look for points through a paragraph or section of the text, you should take care to look at the beginning, the middle **and** the end of the section. Using answer starters like 'To begin with ...', 'As the paragraph progresses ...', 'Towards the

TOP TIP

Underlining or highlighting short key words or phrases in the specified section of the passage can really help when you are summarising. Use a process of elimination to narrow your choices of key point down to the number of marks available.

end …' or 'Finally …' can help to keep you on track to cover the whole section without missing key points.

Study the following list, which will help you to memorise the process:

1. Quickly and accurately re-read the relevant section or lines.
2. Look at the number of marks available for the question (often four marks) and do your best to identify a corresponding number of main points. You may wish to annotate, underline or highlight the text in your paper.
3. If you have more points than there are marks available, eliminate any points that are less important or any points that are similar to others.
4. Create a bullet-point answer by paraphrasing or rewording each point into new alternative words of your own.

TOP TIP

Using bullet points to structure your answer to summary questions can help you to home in on the key points, as well as saving you valuable time in the exam.

Build your skills

Here, we will return for a final time to the text about climate change and poverty. Re-read the extract once more, focusing closely now on how the writer moves from one sub-topic or idea to another.

> 1 There is now very little doubt in the minds of rational people that climate change is a real and grave concern. Coral reefs are bleaching. Deserts are expanding. Forests are burning. Our profligate, consumerist culture, our selfish, privileged greed, and our mindless
> 5 egotistical desires are killing the planet we live on and the creatures we share it with. And yet, this most profound problem of our age is closely linked to the other extreme challenge facing millions across the globe: the problem of abject, soul-crushing poverty. How can the estimated 10% of the world's population who are living in extreme
> 10 poverty be expected to consider the environment? People existing on three dollars' income a day or less literally can't afford to be worrying about microplastics, carbon emissions or shrinking glaciers. And the world's poor are those who will bear the brunt of the apocalyptic future effects of climate change, while the rich will be relatively
> 15 insulated from these effects. Something must be done.

Q **Using your own words as far as possible, summarise the main points the writer makes about climate change and poverty in this paragraph. (4 marks)**

Develop your own answer by copying and completing the following table. Once you have finished the task, you can compare your answers with the completed table in *Consolidate your learning.*

Re-read the relevant section.	
Identify the most important/outstanding points made.	
If you have more than four points, eliminate any points that seem repetitive or less important than others.	
Create a bullet-point answer using your own words as far as possible to paraphrase the main points.	

Consolidate your learning

Re-read the relevant section.	Yes
Identify the most important/outstanding points made.	Climate change is very serious. Specific examples include coral reefs, deserts and forest fires. Climate change is the result of our behaviour. Climate change is linked to poverty. Poor people can't be expected to think about climate change. Poor people will suffer most. Rich people will suffer less.
If you have more than four points, eliminate any points that seem repetitive or less important than others.	Eliminate specific examples; eliminate poor people not being expected to think about it; eliminate rich people will suffer less.
Create a bullet-point answer using your own words as far as possible to paraphrase the main points.	• Climate change is a serious problem. • Climate change is the result of human behaviour. • Climate change is linked to poverty. • The poor will suffer the most.

For summarising questions, it is not recommended you write your answer out in full, as there is a danger you will write too much, and your answer may not be clear about the main points. So, an example bullet-point answer to the question would look like this:

- *Climate change is a serious problem* (1 mark)
- *Climate change is the result of human behaviour* (1 mark)
- *Climate change is linked to poverty* (1 mark)
- *The poor will suffer the most* (1 mark)

Candidate question

In the past, teachers have encouraged me to write in full sentences. Do I have to answer in sentences for RUAE?

A No, you don't have to answer in sentences for RUAE. Brief, clear answers are acceptable, as are bullet-point answers. The RUAE paper assesses your abilities in reading, not writing. (But don't forget your writing will be assessed in the critical essay and portfolio parts of the course, and you should always write in full sentences for these parts!)

Checklist for your answers on 'summarising':

1. Re-read or skim over the relevant section.

2. Select one main point per mark available for the question.

3. Eliminate any superfluous minor points.

4. Create a bullet-point answer by paraphrasing or rewording each point.

Looking ahead

Model answers referring to summarising for your reference:
- *Just Grow Up!*, question 10
- *Get Myself Connected*, question 9
- *Egg Terrorists*, question 9.

9 | Questions that ask you about the 'effectiveness of the passage's conclusion'

TOP TIP

How a writer 'leaves' the reader at the end of a piece of writing is very important. You may wish to try out some of the ideas from this section about how writers create effective conclusions as you are drafting your own folio writing.

These questions typically come at the end of the question paper and ask you about the end of the passage. Be aware that while this type of question asks you to look at the end of the passage, you should also think about the whole passage. Put very simply, these questions are asking something like 'How good is the end of the passage?' or 'Which particular examples of language are employed to conclude the passage well?'

How do I do it?

The question is asking you to evaluate how well the last part of the passage rounds off the text, so you do need to refer to some of the main ideas or to the writer's argument or point of view as expressed throughout.

These questions are very open and there are usually a range of different possible answers. It is worth remembering that you may refer to any examples of language that you might spot in the conclusion, so if there is an interesting image, feature of sentence structure or choice of word that helps to complete or round off the passage, this might be worth commenting on.

Sometimes, the writer may return to an idea from the beginning of the passage, rounding the passage off and giving us the sense that the discussion has come 'full circle'. Again, if this happens, it is worth commenting on in your answer. You can rest assured that the passage will be concluded effectively, and that there will be something you can spot in the language or ideas at the end of the passage that is worth commenting on.

KEY CONCEPTS

Conclusion in simple terms means the ending, but it also suggests a carefully reasoned judgement after a period of thought.

Your approach to answering questions on the effectiveness of the conclusion should be the same as your approach to answering any of the other questions on examples of language, with one added requirement – you need to link what you say to one or more of the main ideas expressed elsewhere in the text.

Study the following list, which will help you to remember how to approach these questions:

1. Re-read the relevant section.
2. Identify expressions which you might choose, thinking of the ideas covered or the examples of language present.

3. Select the most promising example.
4. Briefly quote and provide your developed comment, focusing on an idea and/or an example of language (while taking care to refer to one or more of the main ideas of the passage as a whole).

Build your skills

The following paragraph is the conclusion to the passage you have been looking at about climate change and poverty. In this concluding paragraph, the writer imagines a wealthy tourist on a luxury aircraft which is just about to land. Read the paragraph and consider the question that follows it.

1   So, as the wealthy tourist awakes from her comfortable slumber in
     an insulated first-class luxury pod on board the Boeing Dreamliner
     40,000 feet above the Persian Gulf, enjoying a hot shower with water
     which has been transported over the oceans and deserts for her
5   convenience, perhaps choosing her outfit for the day before sipping
     her yuzu juice and consuming her gourmet breakfast, will she glance
     down at the desert far below and give a thought to the impoverished
     farmers there whose livestock are dying from lack of water while
     their crops fail and the fertile land shrinks from beneath their feet?
10   The nightmare fate of the world's poor will be determined by the
     choices of the world's rich.

Q Select any expression from these lines and explain how it contributes to the passage's effective conclusion. (2 marks)

Develop your own answer by copying and completing the following table. Once you have finished the task, you can compare your answers with the completed table in *Consolidate your learning*.

Re-read the relevant section.	
Look for expressions or examples of language that seem to conclude the ideas of the passage well.	
Select the most promising example/idea and make sure you are clear about how it rounds off or concludes one of the main ideas from the passage.	
Create your answer by quoting or referring to your chosen example/idea and commenting on its effectiveness.	

Consolidate your learning

Re-read the relevant section.	Yes
Look for expressions or examples of language that seem to conclude the passage well.	<ul><li>Word choice – 'slumber', 'luxury', 'convenience', 'gourmet' suggest comfort, riches, opulence, (1) linking back to the idea of excess consumption in the rest of the passage (1).</li><li>Very long, complex first sentence builds cumulative impression of wealth (1) before switching to anticlimax of poor farmers below – emphasises poverty through contrast (1).</li><li>Rhetorical question (1) invites us to ask whether the tourist thinks of poor people at all – link to wealth/poverty idea (1).</li><li>Descriptions of drought, dying livestock and expanding desert link to idea of climate catastrophe from earlier in the passage.</li><li>Abrupt, short second sentence (1) links rich and poor together – this seems to be the main theme or idea running through the passage (1).</li><li>Contrasting word choice – 'Dream(liner)' and 'nightmare fate' (1) emphasises poverty again (1).</li></ul>
Select the most promising example/idea and make sure you are clear about how it rounds off or concludes one of the main ideas from the passage.	Sentence structure used to emphasise gap between rich and poor.
Create your answer by quoting or referring to your chosen example/idea and commenting on its effectiveness.	Long and complex rhetorical question ('So, as the wealthy tourist ...') builds cumulative impression of wealth and excessive consumption (1), followed by blunt, direct second sentence ('The nightmare fate ...') emphasising the effects on the poor (1).

So, a developed answer written in full might look like this:

Sentence structure is used to conclude the writer's main ideas about wealth and poverty – a long and complex rhetorical question ('So, as the wealthy tourist ...') (1 mark) builds a cumulative impression of wealth and excessive consumption (1 mark).

The comment above would be sufficient to gain the two marks available. The following would also gain the two marks:

A much shorter second sentence concludes the paragraph bluntly, stating, 'The ... fate of the ... poor will be determined by ... the rich' (1 mark), again linking back to the writer's central idea of poverty and wealth being connected (1 mark).

A concise, bullet-point answer might look something like this:

- *Sentence structure – long, complex, rhetorical question ('So, as the wealthy tourist ...') (1 mark) creates impression of excess and selfishness, linking to earlier idea of selfishness in passage (1 mark), or*
- *Sentence structure – contrasting, shorter final sentence (1 mark) concludes bluntly, 'fate of poor ... determined by the rich', linking back to main theme of passage and concluding effectively (1 mark)*

When I'm in my exam and I'm looking through the text for examples of language or ideas, is it OK for me to underline, circle or highlight parts of the text?

A Yes, absolutely. The exam paper is yours and you should use it as suits you best. Underlining, circling or highlighting is a good strategy to help you identify and 'capture' your ideas as you read. Some candidates like to write the names of language examples in the margin next to where they appear in the text. Later, when you are searching for material for your answers, your annotations may prove to be very useful.

Checklist for your answers on 'effectiveness of conclusion' questions:

1. Short quote chosen and copied into answer. ☐

2. Identify an example of language (imagery, word choice, sentence structure, etc.) and/or identify a key idea from the specified lines. ☐

3. Link back to an idea from the main body of the passage, or from the beginning of the passage. ☐

4. Particularly good answers might also show how the writer's thinking has developed as the passage progresses, or how the conclusion emphasises a key idea or point. ☐

Looking ahead

Model answer referring to 'passage's effective conclusion' for your reference:

- *Get Myself Connected*, question 10.

Example Question Paper 1 – *Just Grow Up!*

In this article the writer describes tennis star Andy Murray's development as a player and a person.

1 He was the surly Scottish kid with the frizzy hair, the skinny frame and the bad attitude. As a young tennis player

5 and one-time rising star of the sport, Andy Murray was portrayed in the media as moody, bad-tempered or even downright aggressive. He was

10 almost impossible to watch. When things were going well, the winning of a Murray point would be celebrated with a visceral roar accompanied by a

15 hateful scowl, while his raised forearm made a pummelling gesture with his closed fist. When things were going badly, it was even worse. The Murray negativity just seemed to feed off itself, like an overheated engine running on its own burning oil. As his match leads began to slip away, it was difficult to feel any sympathy.

20 Like John McEnroe before him, whose bad-tempered outbursts offended sports fans and umpires alike with shocking regularity in the nineteen-eighties, Murray was emerging as a wee bit of a punk in the polite, champagne-and-Armani world of international tennis. His lack of grace became a talking point: he was all testosterone and no charisma; he hogged the PlayStation and guzzled junk food; he was unapologetically dour in press conferences.

25 The polite and well-heeled tennis establishment sort of wanted him to win but didn't quite know how to take him. He seemed to have more potential than the previous Great New Hope for British tennis, Tim Henman, but he was less mannerly than Henman. He offended his supporters south of the border when it was reported he'd said he would support anyone who was playing against England in the football World Cup. To make matters worse, Murray's

30 (usually winning) opponents were the princely Spaniard with the angelic smile, Rafael Nadal, or the Swiss king of tennis, Roger Federer, whose grace and regal dignity put the young Andy Murray to shame.

But our perceptions of Murray were to change in a TV instant. In the summer of 2012, tennis fans watched with bated breath as he made it through the rounds, the semis and eventually

35 into the fabled finals of the quintessential British tennis tournament, the only tournament that really matters in the UK: Wimbledon. The pressure and expectation were immense. Murray met Roger Federer in the final. While it was a great and exciting thing for British tennis fans to see a UK representative reaching the Wimbledon men's final for the first time since 1938, the match itself was pretty uninspiring. The noble Federer slowly and steadfastly crushed his young

40 opponent into the dust.

Had we been fools to dream that the Scot could ever triumph at Wimbledon? In the immediate aftermath of the match, a microphone was thrust into Murray's tired fist, and he was invited to say the customary few words to the crowd and the millions watching at home. He was at

his most vulnerable: physically weak and psychologically drained. His face crumpled, his voice
45 broke, and he was once again painful to watch as he squeaked: *OK, I'm gonna do this, it's not gonna be easy* ... before breaking down completely.

As he sobbed these few tortured words, Andy Murray made us love him. We saw him for the first time as a real human being suffering the agony of defeat. And he emerged with immense humility and dignity as, pulling himself together, he went on to thank his family and his team
50 of supporters with his whole heart. His love and appreciation for his followers and his humble respect for Roger Federer endeared him to us forever.

We may have felt a nagging guilt at having been part of the pressure on him, or for having doubted his sincerity. We saw the real Andy Murray and understood him properly for the first time. We noticed how he had filled out. He had gone into his first Wimbledon final a boy and
55 emerged as a man. Andy Murray dried his eyes and returned to training with a new sense of purpose, and a new respect in the eyes of the world.

And his defeat at Wimbledon in 2012 was a kind of victory. It was a victory over the elements within the media that had tried to portray him falsely. It was a victory in that he had learned how far he still had to come; how hard he still had to train. He steeled himself and became
60 more disciplined than ever before. The rest of 2012 became his year as he went on to take a thrilling Olympic gold for Team GB in August and then, finally, to win his first Grand Slam title at the monumental United States Open in September.

Andy Murray had arrived, proving that the negative press he had received as a youngster was wrong, proving perhaps that the media and the public expect far too much of the young.
65 Murray has now taken his rightful place among a generation of British sporting superstars that includes Hannah Cockroft, Jessica Ennis, Mo Farah, and Ellie Simmonds. These are the true celebrities of our age – worthy role models who have shown us dedication, determination, humility and, above all, true maturity.

Questions

Total Marks – 30

Attempt ALL questions

1. Look at lines 1 to 18.

Using your own words as far as possible, summarise why Andy Murray was not always popular as a young player.

You should make **four** key points in your answer.

4

2. Look at lines 1 to 18.

By referring to **one** example of word choice and **one** example of sentence structure, explain how the writer creates a negative impression of Andy Murray.

4

3. Look at lines 17 and 18.

By referring to **one** example of language, show how the writer creates the impression that Andy Murray had lost control.

2

4. Look at lines 22 to 26.

Using your own words as far as possible, what does the writer suggest about tennis fans/the 'tennis establishment'?

You should make **two** key points in your answer.

2

5. Look at lines 29 to 32, the sentence beginning 'To make matters worse ...'.

By referring to **one** example of word choice and **one** example of imagery, show how the writer creates a positive impression of Andy Murray's opponents.

4

6. Look at lines 33 to 40.

Using your own words as far as possible, explain the attitude of the British public to the Wimbledon tournament, and how the 2012 final failed to live up to their expectations.

2

7. Look at lines 33 to 40.

By referring to **two** examples of word choice, explain how the writer makes clear the difference between the public expectations and the reality of the 2012 final.

2

8. Look at lines 47 to 56.

Using your own words as far as possible, explain what the writer's attitude is to Andy Murray at this point in the passage and explain how the attitude of the public changed towards him following his defeat in 2012.

You should make **four** key points in your answer.

4

9. Look at lines 57 to 62.

Using your own words as far as possible, explain the two ways in which Murray's defeat might be considered a 'victory'.

You should make **two** key points in your answer.

2

10. Think about the whole article.

In your own words as far as possible, summarise the key points the writer makes about how the media has influenced the way we view Andy Murray.

You should make **four** key points in your answer.

4

[END OF QUESTION PAPER]

Model Answers 1 – *Just Grow Up!*

1. Any four of the following points would gain you marks:

   People didn't like how he looked: his hair stuck out and he was not muscular (1).

   He seemed to have a negative, aggressive attitude (1).

   He came across as grumpy (1).

   He was sometimes rude (1).

   He didn't fit in with the world of tennis (1).

   He was immature (playing the PlayStation) (1).

   He didn't take his fitness as seriously as he should have (eating poor quality food) (1).

2. Word choice:

   'scowl' (1) is a particularly negative-sounding word, suggesting bad temper or anger (1).

   'pummelling' (1) suggests violence and aggression (1).

   'punk' (1) has a harsh sound (with its 'k' consonant) and suggests someone who is non-conformist or unpleasant (1).

   The verb 'hogged' (1) suggests selfishness (1).

   'guzzled' (1) suggests uncouth manners (1).

   Sentence structure:

   In paragraph one, the writer uses two three-part structures (1) to build up a cumulative negative impression (1) ('the frizzy hair, the skinny frame and the bad attitude' and 'moody, bad tempered or even downright aggressive').

   The second sentence in paragraph two uses a colon (1) to expand on the idea of his 'lack of grace' (1), before listing three examples (1) of things people didn't like about him. The three-part rhetorical structure is powerful in building up a negative impression (1).

3. The image 'like an overheated engine' (1) compares Andy Murray to an engine that is running out of control. As the engine keeps running on the burning oil, Andy Murray would keep going on his own negativity. The simile suggests unbearable heat, and things going out of control (1), becoming dangerous, damaged and unstoppable (1).

4. Well-mannered (1)

   Rich/well-off (1)

   Fashionable (1)

5. Word choice:

'princely' (1) suggests that Rafael Nadal looks handsome and has good manners (1). The word also suggests that he might be honourable (1).

'angelic' (1) is a particularly positive adjective to describe Nadal's smile and suggests that he has graceful or youthful good looks, like an angel (1). It implies that he is charming, perfect, beautiful, virtuous (1).

Imagery:

Federer is described in a metaphor as the 'king of tennis' (1). This suggests that he is the ultimate ruler, a mature man at the height of his powers (1). The word 'king' also has connotations that suggest he is honourable (1).

6. The British public feel that Wimbledon is by far the most important/most prestigious/most exciting tournament in the world (1).

The 2012 final was quite a boring match, as Federer slowly but surely defeated Murray (1).

7. 'fabled' (1) suggests that stories have been told about Wimbledon for generations (1).

The word 'quintessential' (1) implies that there is nothing else quite like Wimbledon: it is unique; it is the 'essence' of British tennis (1).

'Uninspiring' (1) is a contrast to the words above and tells us that the match was not good entertainment (1).

There is an anticlimax (1) where it states that Murray was 'crushed' by Federer. 'Crushed' sounds particularly strong and powerful, showing that Murray was very soundly beaten (1).

8. The writer's attitude is one of sympathy, admiration, respect (1).

The public realised they had been wrong about him (1); felt guilty about having been negative (1); learned the truth about him (1); began to admire him (1).

9. He had a victory over the press, who had given people the wrong impression of him (1).

He conquered his own negativity and realised how hard he really had to work to win (1).

10. Any of the following points would gain marks here:
   - Firstly, the media picked up on his negativity on the tennis court (1).
   - They focused on his personality and tried to make people think he was bad tempered and immature (1).

- Later, the media unwittingly gave him the opportunity to prove this negative portrayal wrong (1).
- The writer suggests some aggression when it says a microphone was 'thrust' into his fist at Wimbledon 2012 (1). Here, the media broadcast Andy Murray talking from the heart, and people supported him (1).
- Finally, his eventual successes on the court showed that the media had been wrong about him (1).
- The media had expected too much of him when he was very young (1).
- He proved them wrong about his negativity; he proved himself to be a great tennis player (1).

Example Question Paper 2 – *Get Myself Connected*

In this article the writer reflects on Scottish traditional music of the past and the present.

1   A bitter, wet January wind blows in off the river Clyde. It swirls heavy rain through the illustrious city centre streets and across the

5   doorways of the various historic pubs, theatres and concert halls that serve as the venues for Glasgow's annual *Celtic Connections* traditional music festival.

10 Of all the great Scottish cities, perhaps only Glasgow could pull this off in the darkest depths of the northern winter. Glasgow has the brassy confidence, the gallus determination, and – let's face it – the pure and simple insatiable

15 appetite for a party that are required to stage one of the warmest, loudest, and most energetic trad festivals on Earth.

For 18 days and nights each winter this city rocks – there's no other word – to the thrilling and exotic sounds of the cream of the world's trad talent. It's not unusual for there to be acts representing five different continents at *Celtic Connections*. And trad music's not what you

20 might think it is. It is crushingly loud, and thrillingly electric. It is raucous song and wild dance. It is lit with vibrant colour washes. Trad is young, and trad is cool.

It wasn't always this way. Going back 40 years or so, it seemed trad music was played only by stereotypically bearded men in grubby knitted jerseys. It was confined to the smoky back rooms of dingy pubs. Wheezing penny whistles and squeaky fiddles provided the

25 accompaniment for incomprehensible and obscure lyrics about Scotland's past. Few listened. Trad music itself had become something of a cultural 'back room'. It was older and it was rural, and it was the complete opposite of the mainstream popular culture, the hip rock and cool urban pop music of those times. Trad, in the seventies and eighties, was not the music of the popular set.

30 But what many failed to realise about the folk players and singers of the seventies and eighties was that these musicians were vital to the continuation of our rich musical and lyric traditions. They were the few remaining living links to the great music of Scotland's past.

These were the people who knew the tunes of the great Perthshire fiddler and contemporary of Robert Burns, Niel Gow, or the Victorian Strathspey fiddle king, James Scott Skinner. They

35 sang the radical political folk songs of Scotland's urban industrial age. They understood the virtuosity of twentieth-century accordionist Jimmy Shand. They knew by heart the ancient ballads of the North East or the Borders. They felt in their souls the stirring Nordic fiddle styles of Orkney and Shetland, or the heartbreaking Gaelic songs of the Highlands and Western Isles. In short, these players and singers contained and carried Scotland's music forward for us today.

40 One regular act at *Celtic Connections* that epitomises the way contemporary folk music blends old and new is Orkney trad supergroup *The Chair*. *The Chair*'s particular brand of trad is known

as 'stomp'. It's loud and energetic, and incorporates dub and blues influences against a solid traditional Scottish background. As you might imagine, there's always plenty of enthusiastic dancing at a *Chair* gig.

I met up with founder members Gavin Firth and Douglas Montgomery over a cappuccino in Glasgow's *Park Bar* to ask them about how *The Chair* manages to move their music forward without forgetting their roots.

'One of the tracks on our latest album is a nineteenth-century Orkney ballad called *Hammars of Syradale*', says Firth. 'The song was lost and completely forgotten about, before being rediscovered by a recent local archive project. Our version aims to sound fresh and modern, with a driving backbeat and electric instruments. We're proud of the restoration job we've done on the song.' Montgomery talks about an old Orkney fiddle tune that has been reinvigorated on the album: '*The Road to Hammar Chunkie* was first recorded in the nineteen seventies. I would never say our version improves on the original – the original's absolutely fantastic – but modern studio production techniques and electric accompaniments have meant that we've been able to enhance the grandeur and grace of the old tune.'

Whatever the magic is that *The Chair* conjures up, gig-goers old and young alike are loving it. And the combinations of old and young, or old and new, are the key to the future for Scottish trad. Organisers at *Celtic Connections* invest huge amounts of money and energy in community projects to get everyone connected. 70% of Glasgow schoolchildren have had some exposure to traditional music through the festival's programme of free concerts and workshops. Maybe best of all, the Danny Kyle Open Stage award has become an annual highlight. This free event is a competitive showcase for new talent, featuring young or school-aged musicians from all over Scotland. Winning a Danny Kyle award at *Celtic Connections* is *the* way to get yourself noticed, to get yourself connected in the ever-evolving world of trad. *Celtic Connections*, it can safely be said, celebrates tradition and creates opportunities in a fair, democratic and visionary way.

Questions

Total Marks – 30

Attempt ALL questions

1. Look at lines 1 to 10.

   Using your own words as far as possible, explain what impression the writer creates of the city of Glasgow.

   You should make **two** key points in your answer.

   2

2. Look at lines 11 to 17.

   Using your own words as far as possible, explain how the character of the city of Glasgow contributes to the success of the *Celtic Connections* festival.

   You should make **two** key points in your answer.

   2

3. Look at lines 18 to 22.

   By referring to **one** example of word choice and **one** example of sentence structure, explain how the writer creates a positive impression of modern traditional music.

   4

4. Look at lines 22 to 29.

   By referring to **two** examples of language, show how the writer creates a negative impression of traditional music and musicians of the 1970s and 1980s.

   4

5. Look at lines 30 to 32.

   By referring to any part of this sentence, explain how it helps to provide a link between the writer's ideas at this point in the passage.

   2

6. Look at lines 33 to 39.

   By referring to **two** examples of language, show how the writer creates a more positive impression of traditional music and musicians of the 1970s and 1980s.

   4

7. Look at lines 55 and 57.

   Using your own words as far as possible, explain **two** ways in which *The Chair* has modernised old tunes.

   2

8. Look at lines 49 to 57.

By referring to **two** examples of language, show how the musicians' latest project is described in a positive way.

4

9. Look at lines 60 to 67.

Using your own words as far as possible, summarise the key positive aspects of *Celtic Connections* described in these lines.

You should make **four** key points in your answer.

4

10. Look at lines 58 to 67.

Select any expression from these lines and explain how it contributes to the passage's effective conclusion.

2

[END OF QUESTION PAPER]

Model Answers 2 – *Get Myself Connected*

1. The weather is bad (1).

    The city is impressive and grand (1).

2. Glasgow is sure of itself (1).

    Glasgow tries hard (1).

    or

    Glasgow enjoys a celebration (1).

3. Word choice:

    'rocks' (1) has connotations of energy and movement and suggests that the music livens everyone up (1).

    'thrilling' (1) sounds particularly positive, as if the music creates excitement and pleasure (1).

    'cream (of the world's trad talent)' (1) tells us that these are the very finest musicians in the world (1).

    Sentence structure:

    Three sentences begin in the same way with 'It is ...', followed by a positive statement (1). This use of parallel sentence structure creates a cumulative build-up of positive aspects of the festival (1).

    The final sentence ('Trad is young, and trad is cool.') (1) is a short, forceful, blunt statement (1). This sentence has a finality that makes it difficult to argue with. It sounds very assertive and very positive (1).

4. Word choice:

    'smoky' (1) sounds unpleasant and unhealthy and creates a negative impression (1). Similarly, the adjective 'dingy' (1) makes the pubs seem dark and unappealing (1).

    'wheezing' and 'squeaky' (1) both suggest that the music was weak or unpleasant to listen to (1), while 'incomprehensible' and 'obscure' (1) suggest the lyrics were difficult to understand, or that they were meaningless (1).

    Imagery:

    The metaphor comparing trad music to a 'back room' (1) is effective in creating a negative impression. This metaphor makes us think that trad music was hidden away, either because it wasn't worth listening to, or because people didn't want to listen to it (1). We imagine a dark, unpleasant, unfashionable place (1).

Sentence structure:

The particularly short and pithy statement 'Few listened.' (1) seems to sum up the negative image and the problems that trad music had (1).

Other language features:

The writer uses contrast (1) between paragraph three, which is very positive, and paragraph four, which is very negative (1). There is also contrast (1) within paragraph four, where the writer shows the difference between how people viewed trad music and how people viewed rock/pop at the time (1).

5. The sentence mentions the 'folk players of the seventies and eighties'. This links back to the topic of the previous paragraph (1), which is about trad music in those decades (1). Then the paragraph mentions 'the great music of Scotland's past'. This is the link forward (1) to the subject of the next paragraph, which is about the history of Scotland's music (1).

6. Word choice:

The phrase 'felt in their souls' (1) implies that they had a deep emotional connection to the music (1).

'ancient' (1) suggests that the ballads have stood the test of time (1).

'stirring' (1) implies that the tunes have a powerful emotional effect on the listener (1).

'heartbreaking' (1) suggests that the songs are poignant, that they make the listener feel strong emotion (1).

By saying that they 'contained ... Scotland's music' (1) the writer suggests these people were an important part of history (1).

Sentence structure:

The writer uses repetition very effectively (1) to build a cumulative, positive impression of these players (1). Four sentences begin with the pronoun 'They', followed by a positive verb (1), emphasising the players and singers in a positive way (1): 'They sang ... They understood ... They knew ... They felt ...'. These parallel sentence openings (1) create a build-up that ends in the climax of the final, powerful sentence of the paragraph (1): 'these players and singers contained and carried Scotland's music forward for us today'.

7. The use of electric instruments (1).

The use of an up-to-date recording studio (1).

8. The metaphor 'restoration job' (1) compares the way the band have taken an old song and re-worked it to the way a craftsperson might restore something old, like a building or a piece of furniture (1).

    The metaphor (1) suggests that the song was worthwhile and valuable to begin with, and that the band have made a good-as-new version of it (1). They have restored it to its former glory.

    The word 'grandeur' (1) suggests an impressive positive force (1) and the choice of the word 'grace' (1) makes us think of an elegant sound or movement (1).

9. *Celtic Connections* works with the community in the city (1).

    Most Glasgow schoolchildren are involved in the festival one way or another (1).

    The Danny Kyle award gives young musicians the chance to show their talent (1).

    Celtic Connections mixes old and new and helps young musicians (1).

    or

    Celtic Connections aims to help as many people as possible (1).

10. 'The way to get yourself noticed, to get yourself connected' – the writer uses repetition (1) to focus on the individual person gaining exposure (1).

    or

    The writer returns to the idea from the title of the passage (1) that music is about 'connection' (1).

    or

    'The ever-evolving world of trad' suggests (1) the tradition is in good health and will continue (1); suggests the tradition is always changing and renewing itself (1).

    or

    'celebrates tradition and creates opportunities in a fair, democratic and visionary way' (1) – this is a fitting, positive close to the passage, which has focused on the positive effects of traditional music and *Celtic Connections* for everyone involved (1).

Example Question Paper 3 – *Egg Terrorists*

In this article the writer describes their love of wild birds' eggs and the conservation measures taken to protect nests and eggs.

1 What exactly is it about the eggs of wild birds that fascinates and captivates us? Think of the fragile eggs of
5 our smallest bird, the tiny goldcrest, that appear like a cluster of luminous pearls in a cup-shaped nest made of cobwebs, slung beneath the
10 highest branch of a windswept Dumfries pine. Or imagine the nest of a ptarmigan with its clutch of miraculously warm eggs, hidden among patches
15 of lingering spring snow, high in the mountains of Assynt. Or the mottled, cryptically camouflaged eggs of the Arctic tern that appear suddenly at our feet on a beach walk in Fife.

I'll never forget the sudden shock of delight I felt at 12 years old on parting the bracken to reveal seven flawless blue mallard eggs nestling on a bed of down beside a burn in the
20 Campsie Fells; the smooth blue was such a contrast to the rough natural browns and greens all around in the landscape. Whether they are the eggs of an exotic wild bird, or just those of a common suburban visitor like a robin, wren or blue tit, they all somehow capture our human imagination.

Birds' eggs are everywhere in our art, mythology and folklore. The Fabergé Eggs, crafted by
25 master jewellers for Russian aristocrats in the late nineteenth and early twentieth centuries, are some of the most beautiful, ornate and valuable man-made objects in existence. But somehow, they are less special than real eggs. Folk tales of birds laying golden eggs may remind us of a time when we were poorer, and closer to nature. But again, for me, the material wealth offered by the golden egg is somehow of more limited worth than the natural miracle
30 of the real bird's egg. The real egg is beautiful, tactile and bursting with potential energy in a way that no man-made egg can ever match. The real egg is a true miracle of biology, genetics and evolution.

So why should it be that people steal eggs from the nests of wild birds? The appeal of the egg is plain to see. But for some, simply seeing the egg is not enough. Seventy years ago,
35 collecting wild birds' eggs was the pastime of many an adventurous youngster in the Scottish countryside.

As a child, I remember seeing a glass display cabinet that had belonged to my great uncle. It contained around fifty eggs that he had collected when he was a boy. There were the eggs of falcons, wading birds, finches and even cliff-nesting species like razorbills and guillemots.
40 How dangerous it must have been for him to reach those precarious nests! Each egg had a tiny pin-prick hole at either end where it had been deliberately punctured, before the yolk and the

white were 'blown' out. When my great uncle was a youngster, few saw anything wrong with collecting eggs. In those days, however, wild birds were more abundant, and their habitats were more extensive.

45 Now, things are very different. An egg collection like the one I saw all those years ago could easily land the owner in prison. And rightly so. While I can understand the appeal of collecting (up to a point) I also understand that wild birds are under more pressure than ever before from a host of human evils, including destruction of their habitats, persecution on their migration routes, illegal poisoning and the accumulation of deadly pesticides in their bodies. Birds didn't
50 ask for us to interfere in their millions-of-years-old existence, and now they need all the help they can get from us.

And egg collectors these days are not boys but grown men. They are highly skilled and professional criminals who use military reconnaissance techniques and expensive specialist equipment to rob, plunder and steal. Some even take eggs to order. They have a compulsive
55 and obsessive desire to collect eggs; a twisted psychological disorder. The rarer the bird, the more desirable its egg becomes to these unscrupulous wildlife terrorists.

But there is also a growing band of determined individuals who give their time and energy to combat the egg thieves. In the 1950s, when rare ospreys returned to nest in Scotland for the first time in nearly forty years, a small group of hardy amateur birdwatchers worked months
60 of gruelling shifts to guard the first vulnerable nests from egg thieves. Their story has become part of conservation legend. Police Scotland now employs dedicated and highly trained wildlife crime officers, whose job it is to deal with crimes like the illegal poisoning of birds of prey, the destruction of rare freshwater pearl mussels, or the theft of wild birds' eggs. And the RSPB – the leading charity for the preservation and protection of wild birds – has gone to the
65 lengths of having its staff trained by British Army Gurkhas in the techniques of camouflage, surveillance and radio skills; all of this to ensure the safe, successful and natural hatching of birds' eggs. We should feel confident and optimistic that one day the odious crime of egg theft will become a thing of the past.

Questions

Total Marks – 30

Attempt ALL questions

1. Look at lines 1 to 3.

    Using your own words as far as possible, explain how the writer feels about the eggs of wild birds.

    You should make **two** key points in your answer.

    2

2. Look at lines 4 to 17.

    By referring to **two** examples of language, explain how the writer creates the impression that the birds' eggs are special.

    4

3. Look at lines 27 and 28.

    Using your own words as far as possible, explain why, according to the writer, folk tales refer to golden eggs.

    You should make **two** key points in your answer.

    2

4. Look at lines 30 to 32.

    Using your own words as far as possible, explain why the writer finds real eggs so appealing.

    You should make **four** key points in your answer.

    4

5. Look at lines 43 and 44.

    Using your own words as far as possible, explain why taking wild birds' eggs was considered less of a crime seventy years ago.

    You should make **two** key points in your answer.

    2

6. Look at lines 48 and 49.

    Using your own words as far as possible, summarise what each of the 'human evils' is.

    You should make **four** key points in your answer.

    4

7. Look at lines 52 to 56.

By referring to **two** examples of language, explain how the writer makes clear their view of the egg thieves.

4

8. Look at lines 57 to 61.

By referring to **two** examples of language, explain how the writer makes clear their view of those who work to protect the birds.

4

9. Think about the whole passage.

In your own words as far as possible, summarise four key points the writer makes about the appeal of eggs, the history of egg collecting and the efforts that have been made to protect birds and their eggs from thieves.

You should make **four** key points in your answer.

4

[END OF QUESTION PAPER]

Model Answers 3 – *Egg Terrorists*

1. 'fascinates' – the writer finds the eggs deeply interesting (1).

   'captivates us' – they cannot stop thinking about them (1).

2. Imagery:

   'like a cluster of luminous pearls' – the writer compares the eggs to pearls in this simile (1). The simile suggests that the eggs are small, beautiful, smooth and very valuable (1).

   Sentence structure:

   The writer opens the passage with a question (1) designed to introduce the topic and engage our interest (1).

   The question (1) assumes that we are 'fascinated and captivated' by birds' eggs (1).

   The writer uses the pronoun 'us' (1) to include the reader and the writer (1).

   The writer begins each of the following sentences describing the eggs with a command 'Think of ...', 'Or imagine ...' (1) to further persuade us that these eggs are special (1).

   Because three sentences begin in the same way, with a command (1), the paragraph has a powerful cumulative build-up, persuading us that the eggs are interesting and special (1).

   Word choice:

   The use of the verb 'appear' and the adverb 'suddenly' (1) imply that there is something almost magical about the tern's camouflaged eggs (1).

   Other language features:

   The writer creates a contrast (1) between the warmth of the ptarmigan's eggs and the cold mountainside where the nest is situated (1).

3. Because people in the past had less money and dreamed of great wealth (1).

   People had more of a connection to the natural world in the past (1).

4. Real eggs are nice to look at (paraphrase of 'beautiful') (1).

   We want to touch them (paraphrase of 'tactile') (1).

   They turn into live creatures (paraphrase of 'potential energy') (1).

   They are marvellous examples of nature/science (paraphrase of 'miracle of biology, genetics and evolution') (1).

5. There were more birds (paraphrase of 'more abundant') (1).

   The areas where birds lived were larger (paraphrase of 'habitats were more extensive') (1).

6. Places they live are being destroyed (paraphrase of 'destruction of habitats') (1).

   They are killed when moving from one place to another (paraphrase of 'persecution on their migration routes') (1).

   They are deliberately poisoned, which is against the law (paraphrase of 'illegal poisoning') (1).

   They are poisoned by farm chemicals (paraphrase of 'pesticides in their bodies') (1).

7. The writer has a deeply negative view of egg thieves.

   They are compared in a metaphor to 'terrorists' (1). I think this metaphor is a slight exaggeration, because terrorists commit crimes against people, whereas egg thieves harm wildlife. The metaphor does, however, give us the impression that they work in a military way, and that their crimes are particularly bad (1).

   Word choice:

   'plunder' verb (1) has negative connotations of taking what isn't yours. It suggests a predatory approach and makes me think of Vikings or an invading army (1).

   'twisted' (1) implies that they think the thieves' minds are distorted, they are not normal people (1).

   Sentence structure:

   The second sentence in the paragraph is particularly long and culminates in a powerful three-part rhetorical climax: 'rob, plunder and steal' (1). This is a good example of tautology, where the writer uses three words with essentially the same meaning to create a dramatic effect (1).

8. They admire the conservationists and have a positive view of them.
   Word choice:
   'combat' (1) – verb suggests they are willing to fight (1).
   'hardy' (1) – adjective connotes strength and determination (1).
   'gruelling' (1) – implies that their work was very hard, that it was physically and emotionally draining (1).
   'vulnerable nests' (1) suggests the fragility of the small population of birds (1).
   'conservation legend' (1) may be a deliberate exaggeration or hyperbole, comparing these conservationists to the heroes of ancient stories (1).

9. Any of the following points would gain marks here:
   The writer begins by showing why they find birds' eggs fascinating (1).
   They love the nests and the eggs themselves and think that they are miraculous and almost magical (1).
   They appreciate the scientific wonder of birds' eggs (1).
   They move on to the topic of egg collecting and begin by explaining that this was once an acceptable pastime (1).
   They explain why egg collecting is no longer acceptable, detailing the dangers wild birds face these days (1).
   They then go on to describe the lengths that people go to in order to steal eggs (1).
   They finish off the article by praising the people who protect the birds and making a positive prediction about the future for birds (1).

Part 2

Critical Reading

Critical Reading: What is it?

The Critical Reading part of your National 5 course is where you study literary texts in class and later demonstrate your knowledge of them in an examination.

This part of the course is known as 'Critical' Reading because, as well as understanding these texts, you are also required to analyse some of the language used by the writers and evaluate the texts.

'Criticism', when we are discussing literature, is not necessarily negative, but it is always evaluative. Your criticism of the texts should be based on strong knowledge and careful thought.

KEY CONCEPTS

A **literary text** is an accomplished, high-quality piece of creative writing, such as a play, poem, novel or short story. Literary texts are considered to be works of art in the same way that sophisticated pieces of music, sculptures or paintings are works of art.

1 | *Section 1: Scottish texts*

There are two parts to Critical Reading.

The first part involves reading and learning about a **Scottish literary text** (or a group of shorter Scottish texts) and answering a series of questions in the exam on an extract from this text or group of texts. The Scottish text you study will be selected from a pre-published 'set' list of high-quality, well-known Scottish texts which have been identified by teachers, young people and assessment specialists as being suitable for study at National 5 level.

The main skills being tested in the Scottish texts part of the course are:

*   summarising (of ideas, characterisation, story events or 'narrative') using your own words as far as possible
*   analysing language such as word choice, sentence structure, imagery, punctuation or the structures of the texts you have studied
*   analysing how the writer uses language to create a particular mood or atmosphere

Robert Burns was a famous 18th-century Scottish poet.

- evaluating the text as a whole: What is the text telling us? What does the text say or mean to you? How has the text influenced your thinking?
- linking the extract in the exam paper to the rest of the text or to other texts (if you have studied a group of shorter texts)

Many of these skills are similar or identical to those you have been developing for the RUAE paper.

Some of the Scottish set texts are contemporary (this means they have been written recently) while others are classics of twentieth-century Scottish literature. Some of the texts are even older, pre-twentieth-century Scottish classics. Scotland has a very rich literature going back through the centuries and many Scottish writers and texts are internationally famous. Teachers, parents and assessment experts agree that it is good for young people to learn about literature originating from the place where they live, and you may find your own life experiences and knowledge help in your study and understanding of these texts.

Scottish texts key data

Text type	Poetry, prose fiction (short novels, extracts, short stories) or drama
Length of text	Ranges from groups of short lyric poems to longer extracts of prose upwards of 30,000 words. Text to be studied in advance of the exam.
Is the text printed in the exam paper?	An extract from the text is printed in the exam paper, but you also need to be able to quote from and refer to the rest of the text(s).
Time to complete	Approximately 45 minutes
Number of questions	Four or five; the final question is worth 8 marks
Number of marks available	20 marks
Percentage of the total marks available for National 5 English	20%

2 | Section 2: Critical essay

The second part of Critical Reading – the 'critical essay' – involves reading and learning about a **different text**, again during class time, and answering one question from a choice of previously unseen essay questions that appear in the exam paper. So, for this part, you will be writing an essay about another text you have studied in class. The text may be poetry, prose fiction or prose non-fiction, or it may be a drama text. Some classes study film or TV drama for this part of the course, and very occasionally a class will study a language topic. There are two unseen essay questions to choose from for each of poetry, prose, drama, film and TV drama, and language. There are no restrictions on which texts can be studied for the critical essay, and no set list of texts for this part of the paper, so teachers and classes are free to choose any good quality text they wish.

The critical essay part of your course may give you an opportunity to study classic or contemporary texts from UK or English literature, or from literature from elsewhere in the world. So, your studies for the critical essay can balance and complement your studies for the Scottish text and give you the opportunity to explore literature from other places. Your teacher may be able to offer you and your class some input into which text(s) are chosen for study in this part of the course.

The assessment for the critical essay takes a different form from the question-and-answer style paper you will complete for the Scottish texts, and you should be aware that your **writing** is being assessed in this part of the exam as well as your **reading** of the text.

The main skills being assessed in the critical essay part of the course are:

- your ability to understand a reasonably complex literary text or texts, and to be able to say what the main ideas or themes of the text are
- your ability to quote from the text and refer to the text, discussing some of the literary techniques or features of language used by the writer
- your ability to write clearly and well, structuring an essay that answers the question you have chosen

The Critical Reading paper is worth a total of 40 marks: 20 marks are available for the Scottish texts section, and 20 marks are available for the critical essay.

KEY CONCEPTS

When we write about the **theme** or **themes** of a literary text, we mean the important, recurrent idea or ideas that the text focuses on, explores and invites us to consider. So, for instance, the themes of Harper Lee's famous twentieth-century novel *To Kill A Mockingbird* include justice, poverty and racism.

Critical essay key data

Text type	Most commonly a novel, drama or poetry; can also be short fiction, film or TV drama, or language
Length of text	Ranges from short lyric poems through to longer texts such as novels or plays
Will I have access to the text in the exam?	No, you must study your text in detail before the exam and be able to quote from and refer to it
Time to complete	Approximately 45 minutes
Number of questions	Two question options per genre (drama, prose, poetry, etc.) but you must choose **one question only** for your answer
Number of marks available	20 marks
Percentage of the total marks available for National 5 English	20%

Candidate question

Will I drop marks in the critical essay if I misspell some words?

A You should always try to spell correctly as far as possible, and you may wish to make a special effort to learn how to spell any technical, new or tricky words you might want to include as you prepare for the exam. You won't be unduly marked down for a small number of spelling errors. As a rule, it is better to include the names of concepts or literary techniques than to leave them out for fear of misspelling them.

KEY CONCEPTS

Genre means the category to which the text belongs. This book deals with the three most studied genres: poetry, prose and drama.

Poetry is usually arranged as a verse or verses on the page. Poetry tends to use a good deal of imagery, and, because it also uses sound effects and rhythms, it is sometimes considered to be closer to song or music than the other genres. The language of poetry is rich and condensed, and it often requires particularly careful reading and consideration to arrive at an understanding.

Prose is simply literary writing that appears in full sentences and paragraphs, as opposed to poetry (which is written in **verses** or **stanzas**) or drama (which is written in **dramatic script**). Novels and short stories are almost always written in prose, apart from a rare sub-genre known as the 'verse novel'. Prose can be fiction (novels or short stories) or non-fiction (i.e. writing about the real world, such as the texts used in the RUAE paper).

The term **drama** is used to describe writing which is designed to be acted out on the stage as a play. Plays are written out in what is known as 'dramatic script'. Dramatic script is easily recognisable because the characters' names are given at the left-hand side of the page and stage directions are included to help the people producing the play to understand the characters' actions and/or attitudes.

Candidate question

I like to read non-fiction and texts about real things that exist in the world, but I find it hard to enjoy poetry or fiction because I know it is just made up.

A Yes, many people feel this way! Some people can find it hard to enjoy literature knowing it is imaginative or invented. It can help if you try to remember that good creative writing or fiction always contains certain truths, observations or insights into human behaviour and human life. Fiction, poetry and drama are designed to entertain us, and also to teach us and to encourage us to think more deeply about things.

For many people, the study of literature at National 5 through the Critical Reading element of the course marks the beginning of a lifetime of reading and enjoyment of incredible texts created by great writers in Scotland and across the world. As a by-product of your reading, you will learn much about history, culture and society, and you will learn to appreciate in more detail the meticulous craft and skills that have gone into the production of some of our great literary works.

Critical Reading: How to do it

This section of the book gives general advice on how you should revise and prepare for the Critical Reading examination paper.

1 | Section 1: Scottish texts

For the **Section 1 Scottish texts** part of the paper, this book provides one set of example questions for each of the 12 set texts, and a set of 'model' or example answers to go with each set of questions. To revise and prepare for the Scottish texts, you will want to browse through later stages of this section to find the text(s) that you have studied and look closely at the relevant example question and answer materials. You will probably wish to write answers to the questions yourself first, and then proceed to look at the example answers, comparing these to what you have written. Before you proceed to these text-specific examples, though, you should work through the following section, which will help you to develop your own answers to the questions on your Scottish text.

Success criteria for Scottish texts section

There are four main things you should aim to do as you write about your Scottish text(s).

1. Show that you have a very good knowledge of the text – both of the extract in the exam paper and of the rest of the text(s).
2. Show that you understand clearly the main ideas or themes of the text, or group of texts.
3. Show that you are able to analyse the writer's use of language and/or features of the genre in the extract given.
4. Show that you can make links between the extract in the paper and other parts of the text. Or, in the case of poetry or short stories, make links between the example given and the other specified poems or stories.

Study these success criteria until you have memorised them. You will do well if you are clear about what is being looked for by examiners. Look for examples of these criteria in the example materials that follow.

For the Scottish texts, some of the questions will test your ability to read closely and analyse the text. If you have covered the text in detail in class, you will know a lot already about the various techniques the writer uses in the extract.

TOP TIP

If a question happens to ask about something that you haven't been taught, or something that seems new to you, don't panic: transfer the skills you have been developing for RUAE, and make the best attempt you can to answer.

'Examples of language' questions and 'summarise' questions

The commonest question type in the Scottish texts section is very similar to a question type you have already learned about for RUAE. This question asks you to identify a feature or features of language and go on to explain the effect of your chosen feature(s). This question typically looks like this:

> **Q** By referring to **two examples of language**, explain how the writer/poet makes it clear/creates a sense of ... **(4 marks)**

So, to answer this question, you will have to do the following things:

1. Quickly re-read the relevant section.
2. Consider which features of language are present in the specified lines of the text.
3. Identify what seems to you to be the two most promising features of language.
4. Quote and identify the first feature, followed by your comment.
5. Quote and identify the second feature, followed by your comment.

These questions are relatively open, and a wide range of features is available for you to comment on. There are a number of additional or specialised features of language that apply when studying drama or poetry, and you ought to refer to some of these if you can. In drama, for instance, you might refer to stage directions or an example of dramatic irony. In poetry, you might refer to imagery, rhyme, rhythm or where the line breaks. For prose, you might be discussing characterisation, sentence structure or imagery.

Occasionally, you may come across a question in the Scottish texts paper which asks you to summarise. The advice for how to answer this question is identical to what you have learned for RUAE. To recap briefly, you should identify the key ideas or points made through the specified section of the text, paraphrase or reword these key points into new words of your own, and list them as a brief bullet-point answer, remembering to include one bullet point per mark available.

Build your skills

For this exercise, start by reading the poem 'Trouble is not my middle name' by Liz Lochhead, which is printed below. The poem is a dramatic monologue, adopting the point of view or voice of a teenager who has found themselves in serious trouble. In the poem, the speaker appeals to a listening adult for compassion and understanding.

Trouble is not my middle name

1   Trouble is not my middle name.
    It is not what I am.
    I was not born for this.
    Trouble is not a place
5   though I am in it deeper than the deepest wood
    and I'd get out of it (who wouldn't) if I could.

    Hope is what I do not have in hell –
    not without good help, now. Could you
    listen, listen hard and well
10 to what I cannot say except by what I do?

    And when you say I do it for badness
    this much is true:
    I do it for badness done to me before
    any badness that I do to you.

15 Hard to unfankle this.
    But you can help me. Loosen
    all these knots and really listen.
    I cannot plainly tell you this, but, if you care,
    then – beyond all harm and hurt –
20 real hope is there.

An example question might look something like this:

Q **Look at lines 1 to 8.**

By referring to two examples of language, explain how the poet creates a sense of crisis. (4 marks)

Develop your answer by copying and completing the following table. Once you have finished the task, you can compare your answers with the completed table in *Consolidate your learning*.

Re-read the relevant section of the text.	
Consider which features of language are present.	
Identify what you think are the two most promising features.	
Quote and identify first feature (1), followed by your comment (1).	
Quote and identify second feature (1), followed by your comment (1).	

Consolidate your learning

Re-read the relevant section of the text.	Yes
Consider which features of language are present.	Placing of concept 'Trouble' at opening of poem. Contradiction/reversal of the cliche 'Trouble is not my middle name'. Simple, short, direct lines. Quickening rhythm and longer lines 'though I am in it deeper …' intensifies the sense of the depth of the trouble. Rhyming couplet at end of stanza emphasises the young person's desire to get out of trouble. Second verse begins (ironically) with the word 'Hope'. Question 'Could you listen …' seems vulnerable, repetition of 'listen' suggests desperation. 'what I cannot say except by what I do' shows they have expressed their trauma through actions, possibly getting themselves into serious trouble; rhyme emphasises this.
Identify what you think are the two most promising features.	Opening poem with concept/word 'Trouble'. Intensifying sense of crisis through rhythm and rhyme in lines beginning 'though I am in it …'.
Quote and identify first feature (1), followed by your comment (1).	Structure/placing of abstract noun 'trouble' (1) at very beginning of poem emphasises sense of crisis (1).
Quote and identify second feature (1), followed by your comment (1).	Intensifying rhythm and rhyming couplet (1) in final two lines of first stanza give impression of deepening crisis (1).

So, a developed answer to the question on page 69, written in full, might look something like this:

The poet has structured the opening carefully to emphasise the word/concept of 'Trouble' (1 mark), *creating an immediate sense of an unfolding crisis* (1 mark).

In the last sentence of the first stanza, the lines become longer, the rhythm quickens and the verse ends in a rhyming couplet (1 mark) *with 'wood' and 'could', intensifying the sense of crisis* (1 mark).

A concise, bullet-point answer to the same question might look something like this:

- *Placing 'Trouble' at very outset* (1 mark) *creates sense of unfolding crisis* (1 mark)
- *Quickening rhythm, rhyming couplet 'deepest wood … I'd get out of it … if I could.'* (1 mark) *creates sense of intensifying crisis* (1 mark).

When you are ready to attempt the questions on your own Scottish text, use the blank table on page 69 to help you to create your answers to questions about examples of language. Once you have written your answers to these questions, compare what you have written to the model answers which appear later in this book, at the end of the section on your chosen Scottish text.

The eight-mark question

The final question of the Scottish texts section always requires a longer, more developed answer. This question will ask you to refer to the text in the exam paper, and to another short text or texts from the specified selection (poetry or short fiction), or part(s) of the text (drama or novel). This is a challenging question and depends on your memory and knowledge of the whole text, or range of poems or stories.

A version of this question appears in every National 5 examination paper, and it is vital you understand how to do it. Eight of the total twenty marks for this part of the paper depend on how well you answer this question. You will realise that it is impossible to do this question without a thorough knowledge of the whole text or group of texts, so you must study your entire text(s) in detail. If you are absolutely clear about how to answer this question, you will feel confident going into your exam.

So, to answer this question effectively you will need to do the following:

1. Identify the thematic focus of the question and think about the extract in your examination paper.
2. Think about the entire Scottish texts selection you have studied (so, the group of poems, the whole play, the specified group of short stories or the whole novel).
3. Identify the link, connection or 'commonality' between the extract in your examination paper and the rest of the text(s). The question will direct you towards this commonality. If you are writing about prose or drama, you will be homing in on one or two key sections of the text other than the extract in the exam paper. If you are writing

KEY CONCEPTS

Don't be put off by the concept of **commonality**, which is used here simply as a shorter way of describing an idea or theme that is shared – or 'common' - across the wider text or pair of texts you are considering.

about poetry or short fiction, you will be writing about one (or more) of the other poems or short stories from the specified selection.

4. State in your answer what or where the commonality is (2 marks).

5. Explore the common idea (the commonality) within the extract. Choose a reference or feature of language and make a comment (2 marks).

6. Explore the common idea (the commonality) across the rest of your text(s). Choose two further references or features of language, quote briefly and make comments (4 marks).

Build your skills

Here, to help you to learn how to answer the eight-mark question, we will use Liz Lochhead's poem 'Trouble is not my middle name' again, and consider it alongside another Scottish poem, a lyric poem by Robert Alan Jamieson called 'We lost us for a while'. **These two poems are not specified texts for National 5 English and will not appear in your examination paper.** They are used here for example and practice purposes only. Robert Alan Jamieson's poem 'We lost us for a while' was written during the height of the Covid-19 pandemic and lockdown.

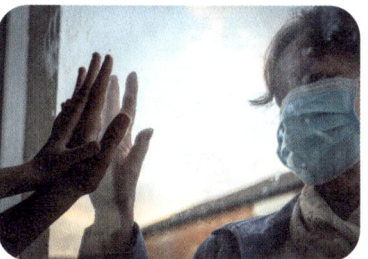

We lost us for a while

1 We lost us for a while

   Until we were ill
   we didn't know how sick our world was.

   Until all was silent
5 we didn't know how noise polluted.

   Until the hospitals were full
   we didn't know how brave the staff are.

   Until the animals came to town
   we thought them dead, or they'd deserted us.

10 Until we saw nobody
   we didn't know the ones we'd miss.

   Some we'll miss forever.

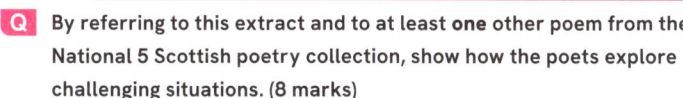

Q By referring to this extract and to at least **one** other poem from the National 5 Scottish poetry collection, show how the poets explore challenging situations. (8 marks)

So, for the purposes of this question, the extract is the first poem 'Trouble is not my middle name', and the one other poem we will use is 'We lost us for a while'.

Develop your own answer by copying and completing the following table with reference to 'Trouble is not my middle name' and 'We lost us for a while'. Once you have finished the task, you can compare your answers with the completed table in *Consolidate your learning*.

Identify thematic focus of question and think about this focus within the given extract.	
Think about the entire Scottish text(s) and make the link between thematic focus of question and other parts of the text(s).	
Quote and comment on commonality or feature of language within given extract (2 marks).	
Identify thematic link or commonality and state where it occurs in the wider text(s) (2 marks).	
Quote and comment on commonality or feature of language elsewhere in the text(s) (2 marks).	
Quote and comment on a second commonality or feature of language elsewhere in the text(s) (2 marks).	

Consolidate your learning

Identify thematic focus of question and think about this focus within the given extract.	Yes – I have considered the idea of the 'challenging situation' in 'Trouble is not my middle name'.
Think about the entire Scottish text(s) and make the link between thematic focus of question and other parts of the text(s).	I have thought about the other texts I have studied and identified another poem that also deals with a 'challenging situation' - it is 'We lost us for a while' by Robert Alan Jamieson.
Quote and comment on commonality or feature of language within given extract (2 marks).	Rhyme emphasising close focus on ideas of care and hope at close of 'Trouble is not my middle name' (1) shows that we can overcome very difficult challenges (1). Final point of Lochhead's poem is one of hope and optimism that '... if you care,/ then – beyond all harm and hurt – real hope is there.'
Identify thematic link or commonality and state where it occurs in the wider text(s) (2 marks).	Another poem from the set list where the poet responds to a challenging situation (1) is 'We lost us for a while' by Robert Alan Jamieson (1).
Quote and comment on commonality or feature of language elsewhere in the text(s) (2 marks).	Overall structure - repetitive series of five reflective couplets (1), each describing a different effect of the pandemic and the challenging circumstances (1), beginning with 'Until', followed by an affirmative response.
Quote and comment on a second commonality or feature of language elsewhere in the text(s) (2 marks).	A forceful, shocking, isolated final line 'Some we'll miss forever' (1), a change in the pattern of the poem, implying the ultimate challenge that friends or family may have died (1).

So, a developed, mini-essay style answer to the question on page 71, written in full, might look something like this:

In the end, Lochhead's poem responds positively to the challenges faced by the young speaker. Although the young person may have committed a crime and be facing serious consequences, the poet shows, using a rhyme to emphasise the words 'care' and 'hope is there' (1 mark)*, that there can be a positive and forward-moving response to the challenges* (1 mark)*.*

Other poems in the Scottish poetry collection deal with challenging situations. The poem dealing with perhaps the greatest challenge is Robert Alan Jamieson's 'We lost us for a while' (1 mark)*, which deals with the enormous challenges of the Covid-19 pandemic and the lockdown* (1 mark)*.*

Jamieson's poem begins with a series of positive, affirmative statements, following the same pattern of using the word 'Until' (1 mark)*, before using enjambment to reveal an aspect of the lockdown or the pandemic in a positive way: 'Until the animals came to town/ we thought them dead ...'. So, the response to the challenge seems positive* (1 mark)*.*

However, the final, shocking, isolated line of the poem – 'Some we'll miss forever' (1 mark) *implies that friends or relatives may have died, showing that the challenge may only just be beginning* (1 mark)*.*

A concise, bullet-point answer to the same question might look something like this:

- *Lochhead shows, using a rhyme to emphasise 'care' and 'hope is there'* (1 mark)*, that there can be a positive and forward-moving response to the challenges* (1 mark)
- *Jamieson's 'We lost us for a while'* (1 mark)*, deals with the enormous challenges of the Covid-19 pandemic and the lockdown* (1 mark)
- *Jamieson begins with a series of positive, affirmative statements, following the same pattern of using the word 'Until'* (1 mark)*, before using enjambment to reveal a positive aspect: 'Until the animals came to town/ we thought them dead ...'. Overall response to the challenge seems positive* (1 mark)
- *However, final, shocking, isolated line – 'Some we'll miss forever'* (1 mark) *implies friends or relatives may have died, shows challenge is only just beginning* (1 mark)

Looking ahead

When a question in the Scottish texts section has a larger number of marks available (typically four or eight marks) you ought to use bullet points in your answer. The model answers which follow later show a mixture of paragraph and bullet-point style answers. The paragraph answers are there to show you the thinking behind the answer, but it is highly recommended you take a bullet-point approach to your answers, especially for those worth four or eight marks. Bullet-point answers can

KEY CONCEPTS
Enjambment is when a line break in a poem comes midway through a sentence, creating a sense of a break in the meaning or the rhythm. Enjambment is often used to create a particular emphasis.

KEY CONCEPTS
Thematic links could be paraphrased simply as 'ideas common to both texts', or 'ideas common to the printed extract and the wider text as a whole'.

be very useful in the exam: they can help you to set out the correct number of main points in your answer for the marks available, and they also free you from the need to write in sentences during this part of your exam. This can save valuable time when you are aiming to complete the Scottish texts section in just 45 minutes. (But remember, your critical essay **must** be written in clear, well-organised, full sentences and paragraphs.)

When you are ready to attempt the questions on your own choice of Scottish text, use the blank table on page 72 to help you to create your answer to the final eight-mark question. Once you have written your answer to this question, compare what you have written to the model answer which appears at the end of the section on your chosen Scottish text.

The example answers given in this book show some very full answers. Don't worry if you don't think you can write as much as is shown in these but do try to ensure that you cover a broad range of points. Look at how these longer example answers make the thematic links between the given text and another text or part of the text. For instance, the answer on 'Love' and 'Strawberries' looks at the significance of human relationships in each poem; the answer on *Death in a Nut* looks at the theme of the supernatural in this text and in *Things My Wife and I Found Hidden in Our House*; the answer on *Yellow Moon* focuses on the theme of masculinity in the extract, and in the play as a whole.

For the **Section 2 Critical essay** part of the paper, this book provides three example critical essays for you to study. These example essays cover the most commonly taught genres of poetry, prose and drama.

For your exam critical essay, you should base your essay answer on the texts you have studied in class – not the texts which are used here for example purposes.

You should also remember that you must choose a different genre in sections 1 and 2. (So you can't write on a poetry text in both sections, for instance, or write both of your answers on prose texts.)

TOP TIP

Remember you *must* choose a different genre in sections 1 and 2 of the Critical Reading paper. So, for instance, if you choose to write about poetry in section 1, you should choose prose or drama in section 2.

Success criteria for critical essay section

There are four main things that you should aim to do as you write your critical essay.

1. Show a very thorough knowledge of your chosen text, its main ideas, central concerns and important details.
2. Using references, quotes and examples from your chosen text, show that you can analyse the writer's use of language and features of the genre.
3. Write an essay that is relevant to your chosen question; write an essay that answers the question.
4. Write an essay that has a clear structure, and uses good, clear, precise English.

Study these success criteria until you have memorised them. You will do well if you are clear about what is being looked for by examiners. Look for examples of these criteria in the example essays that follow.

Choosing your question

Critical essay exam questions for drama, prose and poetry tend to focus on similar things each year. So, drama essay questions tend to focus on either a key character or a key theme. Prose questions also tend to focus on a key character or key theme. Poetry essay questions tend to focus on a broad topic such as the mood or atmosphere created in the poem, or the experience or event described in the poem.

Build your skills

Copy and complete the relevant section of the following table, using your knowledge of the text(s) you have been studying for this part of the course. You should attempt to complete both relevant aspects for each genre you have studied, as this will give you two options for the exam.

Genre	Question area of focus	Specific, relevant aspect of your text
Drama	A key character	
	A key theme or idea	
Prose	A key character	
	A key theme or idea	
Poetry	Atmosphere or mood created	
	Experience explored	

Consolidate your learning

Now compare the entries in your table to the following table, which has been completed using the texts and topics of the example essays which appear later in this book. The topics of the example essays are indicated with an asterisk (*). Other, alternative topics are also given.

Genre	Question area of focus	Specific, relevant aspect of your text
Drama	A key character	The character of Cammy in the play *Black Watch*
	A key theme or idea	*Theme of injustice in the play *Black Watch*
Prose	A key character	*Focus on an 'admirable character' in the novel *To Kill a Mockingbird*
	A key theme or idea	The theme of racism in the novel *To Kill a Mockingbird*
Poetry	Atmosphere or mood created	The atmosphere of festive celebration in Edwin Morgan's poem 'Trio'
	Experience explored	*Focus on the chance meeting in Edwin Morgan's poem 'Trio'

Looking ahead

When you go on to read the example essays, consider how they answer the questions. In each case, the entire essay should be relevant to the question, and the introduction and the conclusion should refer directly back to the question.

Writing your introduction

Your essay should begin with a brief introduction which gives the name of your text and the name of the dramatist, author or poet, as well as pointing out the key aspect of the question you will be addressing in your essay. Your introduction doesn't need to be very long.

Build your skills

Again, copy and complete the relevant row from the following table to help you to draft your introduction.

Genre	Title	Dramatist/author/poet name	Area of focus	Wording of introduction
Drama			Character	
			Theme	
Prose			Character	
			Theme	
Poetry			Atmosphere or mood	
			Experience explored	

Consolidate your learning

Now compare the wording you have come up with to the simplified example introductions from the essays later in this book.

Genre	Title	Dramatist/ author/ poet name	Area of focus	Simplified wording of introduction
Drama	*Black Watch*	Gregory Burke	Theme of injustice	*Gregory Burke's play* Black Watch *deals with the final stages of the history of the Scottish infantry regiment during the Iraq War in 2004. Injustice is a key concern in this play.*
Prose	*To Kill a Mockingbird*	Harper Lee	Admirable character Atticus Finch	*Harper Lee's novel* To Kill a Mockingbird *features an admirable character called Atticus Finch. Atticus is a lawyer in the small town of Maycomb in Alabama. He is the father of Scout Finch, the narrator of the story.*
Poetry	'Trio'	Edwin Morgan	Experience/ chance meeting	*Edwin Morgan's 'Trio' is a poem which begins with a description of a chance meeting and goes on to reflect on deeper ideas suggested by this meeting.*

Topic sentences

Moving on from the introduction, each paragraph or section of your essay should be introduced with a clear 'topic sentence'. This is simply a sentence which identifies and sets out the topic you intend to cover in the paragraph. It should be a simple statement at the beginning of each paragraph before you begin to bring in quotations, examples of language and discussion of these. You might choose to plan a chronological structure for your essay, loosely following the structure of your text.

Build your skills

Study the following table before writing some practice topic sentences of your own, related to the text you are studying. It can be very useful to prepare three or four topic sentences for an essay you may write in future, focusing either on character or theme (for drama or prose) or on experience or mood (for poetry).

Question focus	First topic sentence	Second topic sentence	Third topic sentence
Drama or prose – character	*At the outset, character X appears to be …*	*In the key scene/chapter where …*	*In a later chapter …* or *In the third act of the play …*
Drama or prose – theme	*The theme of X first emerges when …*	*During the key central scene, the author focuses again on the theme of …*	*As the story reaches its climax, we return to the theme of X in a slightly different way …*
Poetry – experience described or mood created	*The atmosphere at the beginning of the poem is clearly one of …*	*As the second verse begins, there is a slight change of focus …*	*The poem concludes by returning to the key idea of …*

Consolidate your learning

Now copy and complete the following table, creating topic sentences of your own, based on the text(s) you have studied. Use and adapt the wordings in the table on page 77 to give you ideas as you learn how to write your own topic sentences.

Question focus	Your first topic sentence	Your second topic sentence	Your third topic sentence
Drama or prose – character			
Drama or prose – theme			
Poetry – experience or mood			

Looking ahead

Now consider the following topic sentences, which have been adapted from the example essays later in this book. These sentences will give you an idea of the overall structure of each example essay.

Question focus	First topic sentence	Second topic sentence	Third topic sentence
Drama or prose – character	*Atticus is a widower, his young wife having died when their children were very small.*	*At almost fifty, Atticus is older than the other fathers in the community …*	*Atticus takes a courageous moral stand when he agrees to defend Tom Robinson …*
Drama or prose – theme	*One important theme in the play is the idea that the soldiers are suffering injustice at the hands of politicians.*	*The play is also concerned with the history of the regiment.*	*The greatest injustice of all, however, comes at the end of the play …*
Poetry – experience or mood	*The poem opens with a description of the chance meeting …*	*From this point on, the poem starts to become much more reflective.*	*This later section of the poem introduces agnostic or humanist ideas, and celebrates the power that human happiness can have …*

TOP TIP

Timing! If you have planned to write three main sections or stages in your essay, and you have 45 minutes to complete it, this gives you approximately 15 minutes to write each section (give or take a few minutes to write a brief introduction and a short conclusion to your essay). It is also a good idea to leave yourself a few minutes at the end to read over and check what you have written.

Essay planning and the 'power of three'

When you have chosen the most appropriate question to suit the text you want to write about, you will next want to briefly plan what your main essay sections will be, which key quotations you will put in each section and which literary techniques or terms you intend to write about in each section.

You have just 45 minutes to write this essay, so it can be a good idea to plan three main sections. Looking ahead, the example essay on 'Trio' follows a three-part plan, covering the positivity of the opening of the poem, the continued positive tone through the middle section and the deeper ideas explored as the poem draws to a close. The example essay on *To Kill a Mockingbird* has three main sections as well: the first looking at the character of Atticus at the opening of the novel, and then the next two looking at how his true character emerges in key scenes in the street and outside the jail. The essay on *Black Watch* is also organised into three main parts – covering the ideas of politics, history and the character of Cammy.

As you plan, don't forget that you must refer to the writer's use of language or use of literary techniques. Look to see how the essay on 'Trio' mentions rhythm, enjambment, dialogue, sound effects and simile. The essay on *To Kill a Mockingbird* covers irony, symbolism, characterisation and metaphor. The essay on *Black Watch* deals with irony, tone, metaphor and stagecraft, including the use of sound and music. You should aim to link your discussion of these techniques back to the question; you can see for instance how the essay on *Black Watch* links these techniques to the key idea of 'injustice' identified by the writer of the essay.

Build your skills

Study the following table, which simplifies the planning process for the essay on 'Trio'.

Essay section (remembering to focus on topic of question)	Which quotes or references will I use?	Which terms, techniques or ideas will I discuss?
Opening stages of poem and positivity	'coming up Buchanan Street' 'the three of them are laughing'	Lively rhythm; enjambment; mood
Middle stages of poem and continuing positivity	'like a teapot holder' 'fresh, sweet cake' 'brisk sprig of mistletoe'	Simile; light-hearted mood; assonance
How the poem moves on to explore deeper ideas towards the end	'the vale of tears' 'whether Christ is born' 'monsters of the year'	Humanism/agnosticism and the power of human happiness

Consolidate your learning

Now copy and complete the following table to make an essay plan for the text(s) you have been studying.

Essay section (remembering to focus on the topic of a question) *You may organise by key scenes, chapters, verses/stanzas, characters, etc. Chronological order can help here.*	Which quotes or references will I use?	Which terms, techniques or ideas will I discuss?

Writing your conclusion

In each of the example essays, a short conclusion rounds off the piece, referring back to the main points covered and using key words from the question again. For 'Trio', the conclusion returns to the ideas of a chance meeting and the deeper ideas covered. For *To Kill a Mockingbird*, the conclusion sums up how our impression of Atticus' heroism has been built up. In the essay on *Black Watch*, the conclusion sums up what the play has to say about the key theme of injustice.

Building your skills

Your conclusion needn't be long, but you should always aim to conclude your essay. If you find yourself running out of time to complete sections you have planned, make sure you make time to write even a very brief conclusion to round your essay off. The following table will help you to plan what to include in the conclusion.

Signal words to indicate you are coming to the conclusion	Reiterate the main argument of your essay and very briefly re-state main points made in each section	Include a strong final statement to sum up your overall point of view on your text
So, to conclude ... In conclusion ... To sum up ... All in all ...	... it is clear that the character of ... ... the theme of X is absolutely central in this text ... ... this poem is very effective in creating an atmosphere of ...	Reading this novel has convinced me that ... Studying this play has made me realise that ... The poet has succeeded in helping readers to see that ...

Consolidate your learning

Now begin to put together a conclusion of your own, based on a text you have studied or are studying, by copying and completing the following table.

Signal words to indicate you are coming to the conclusion	Reiterate the main argument of your essay and very briefly re-state main points made in each section	Include a strong final statement to sum up your overall point of view on your text

Looking ahead

The following table breaks down the conclusion to the example essay on Edwin Morgan's poem 'Trio' to illustrate how to build your final paragraph.

Signal words to indicate you are coming to the conclusion	Reiterate the main argument of your essay and very briefly re-state main points made in each section	Include a strong final statement to sum up your overall point of view on your text
So, ...	... this poem begins with a positive and seemingly simple description of a chance meeting and goes on to reflect on deeper ideas about Christmas and Christianity.	The poem seems to conclude that human happiness and positivity are powerful enough in themselves to overcome pain or adversity that we may face in our everyday lives.

3 | Study tips and advice on how to prepare for Critical Reading

You should read and re-read the key sections of your text(s), or, in the case of shorter texts, you can re-read the entire text. It is **very** important to know your text(s) well, and you should spend a lot of time familiarising yourself with them thoroughly. Read in a quiet place, away from distractions, so that you can **think about the text** and what it means to you.

The better you know your texts, the more confident you will feel about this part of the exam. Although a part of your chosen Scottish text will be reprinted in the exam paper, you do need to know the whole text – or range of texts – very well. For the critical essay, you won't have access to your text in the exam at all, and you must be able to refer to the text in detail, from memory. Get to know your texts so that you feel a sense of ownership of them. If they feel as if they somehow belong to you, then you will enjoy justifying your own views on the texts, and explaining what you think is important in them.

Young people working towards National 5 English are sometimes anxious to know how many quotes they should memorise to prepare for the Critical Reading part of the exam. Unfortunately, it's impossible to put a number on this. However, you can look at the example essays to give you an idea of an appropriate number of quotes or references to include in an essay. Just as important as your quotations are the comments you make about them. Refer to literary techniques used by the writer and discuss the effects of these techniques – what do they make you think?

Remember, you will need to have a broader range than the 10–15 or so references used in the example essays in this book, so that you will be able to deal with whichever topic happens to come up in the unseen questions. It might not be enough to learn 10 or 15 interesting quotes from the character of Cammy in the play *Black Watch*, for instance, because the question in the exam paper might not allow you to focus on just one character. You need to have a breadth of knowledge of your text. You should focus on the parts of the text that you find memorable or interesting and learn a range of short and slightly longer quotes – so you can show your knowledge and understanding.

Write out the quotations you have chosen to learn on a piece of paper, cover it and see if you can re-write them accurately. When you can do this, you will feel confident about your ability to recall them once you are in the exam room. Group your quotes, for instance 'quotes from key character', 'quotes relating to the key theme of …', 'quotes from the beginning of the text' and 'quotes from the closing stages of the text'. Having your quotes and references grouped like this in your mind will help to make sure your essay has clear sections and a logical structure. If you learn better by hearing than reading, it may help you to read out, record and listen again to your key quotations using a phone or computer.

Set aside time to study whichever materials or notes you have to go with your texts themselves, too. Then test yourself against the clock. Take 45 minutes of your time and see if you can pull all your skills and references together into a well-written, logical and relevant essay.

TOP TIP

If the text is a short text like a lyric poem, you can **learn it by heart**. This is easier to do than you might think and will give you confidence going into the exam. Do you know the words to a favourite song? If you do, then you will certainly also be able to learn the words of a poem, some interesting sentences and phrases from a novel or short story, or a soliloquy or set of linked quotations from a play.

TOP TIP

Timing! You have two tasks to complete in Critical Reading (the Scottish texts and the critical essay) and this part of the examination is one and a half hours long in total (unless you have additional time because of dyslexia or another barrier to your learning). You should aim to balance your time carefully and don't use more than about 45 minutes on either part of the paper.

TOP TIP

Planning! It is always important to plan what you intend to write in your essay. This book will help you to learn how to plan an essay. You shouldn't take too long over planning during the exam. It is best if you have a flexible, approximate plan before you get to the exam itself.

When you are in the exam, take care to choose a question for the critical essay that fits your text. The questions will be reasonably broad and are often focused on a character or a theme, but you must be sure that your text really suits the question. If you have chosen a good match between your question and text, you will be able to use key words from the question in the introduction to your essay, in each of your planned main sections and again as you conclude – you should notice that the three example essays do this.

When you are in the exam itself, show off your knowledge and understanding of the text, and include some of your own thoughts and ideas. If you have taken time to think about the text and are able to justify your ideas with references, then you will be able to give a genuine personal response, and you will show your ability in what is known as 'higher order thinking'.

Develop your own ideas about the text by spending some time thinking about what you consider to be the most dramatic, poetic, thought-provoking or memorable point in the text. If you can justify your choice, then you will be thinking deeply, and responding with some of your own ideas.

Copy and complete the following table. This process will help you to develop your personal response to the texts you are studying for the critical essay or Scottish text. Store your completed table somewhere handy and look over it as you prepare for your exam. Try to find an opportunity at some point within your essay to include a reference to your favourite (or most interesting, thought-provoking or dramatic) moment of the text.

Text I'm studying	The most interesting or thought-provoking moment of the text, in my personal view	Short quote and mention of a literary or linguistic technique from this point in the text	My comment or reasoning for selecting this as the most interesting point in the text

Remember that literary texts are written to make us think about important things, and to entertain us. Enjoy your text, make it your own and try to enjoy the experience of writing about it in the exam!

PART A – SCOTTISH TEXT – DRAMA

Text 1 – Drama

If you choose this text, you may not attempt a question on Drama in Section 2.

Read the extract below and then attempt the following questions.

Yellow Moon by David Greig

1 **Lee**   I'm thinking of going into business as a pimp. I don't think there is a pimp in Inverkeithing at the moment. A pimp has to have ho's but I would have does, as in doe a deer. Because I'm Stag Lee.

He has worked out a rap.

5   Stag. S.T.A. double G.
         Big and so hornee.
         Like Bambi's dad. I drive girls mad.

         I think there's room for a pimp in Inverkeithing.
         Roanna Castledine's agreed to be one of my ho's.
10   And so's Kerry Hunter, but I'd still be one ho
         short of the full back seat.

         ...

         What do you say?

         Would you be one of my doe ho's, Silent Leila?

15   There's lassies would give their right arms for some quality time with the Stag man. Check out these abs – (*He lifts his shirt.*) Check that out. I'm a prize.

         Check out these pecs.

         Go on.

Leila feels his heart thump under her hand.

20 She feels his heart beat faster.

And she wonders:

Did I make that happen?

Well did she?

No.

| 25 | **Billy** | Lee. |

It was not beauty that made Lee's heart beat faster.

| | **Billy** | Lee. |

It was not Leila at all.

| | **Billy** | Lee. |

| 30 | It was a jilted amateur boxer with a score to settle. |

| | **Billy** | Where's the ring? |

Billy punches Lee in the stomach.

| | **Billy** | Where is it? |

Billy pushes Lee.

| 35 | **Lee** | Get off. |

Billy pushes Lee again.

| | **Billy** | Where's the bloody ring? |

| | **Lee** | Don't touch me. |

Billy pushes Lee and this time Lee falls.

| 40 | **Billy** | Get up. |
| | | Get up and fight. |

Lee stays down.

| | **Billy** | You think you're hard, Macalinden, but you're all front. You wouldn't last two minutes with me. Two minutes with me and I'd have you wetting your pants. |
| 45 | | Get up. |

Lee stays down.

| | **Billy** | FIGHT |

Billy grabs Lee's hat.

| | **Lee** | Don't touch my hat. |

| 50 | **Billy** | Fight for it. |

| | **Lee** | Give me the hat. |

| | **Billy** | (*mocking*) 'Give me the hat.' |

| | **Lee** | Don't touch my hat. |

| | **Billy** | (*mocking*) 'Don't touch my hat.' |

| 55 | *Lee takes out a knife and stabs Billy.* |

A pause.

Lee stabs Billy again.

Billy drops the hat.

Lee   I told you not to touch the hat.

60 Sometime between midnight and two o' clock in the morning on Saturday 23rd January Billy Logan felt his insides turn into blood and then, at almost the same moment, he felt the blood begin to drain away and his legs buckle beneath him.

Billy   Lee.

Somewhere between midnight and two o' clock in the morning Billy Logan put his hands to
65 his stomach.

His stomach felt wet and warm.

Somewhere between midnight and two in the morning, Billy Logan died and as he died his mind was filled

With these words:

70 Cunt.

You cunt.

You fucking cunt.

Over and over again until the last of his breath was gone.

Questions

1. Look at lines 1 to 15.

    By referring to **two** examples of language, explain how the character of Lee is revealed in the extract.

    4

2. Look at lines 18 to 23.

    By referring to **one** example of language, explain how the writer reveals Leila's thoughts and/or feelings.

    4

3. Look at lines 26 to 45.

    By referring to **one** example of language, show how the writer creates a negative impression of the character of Billy.

    2

4. Look at lines 30 to 55.

    By referring to **two** examples of language, explain how the writer presents the violence in the extract.

    2

5. By referring to this extract and to elsewhere in the play, show how the writer explores the theme of masculinity.

    8

OR

Text 2 – Drama

If you choose this text you may not attempt a question on Drama in Section 2.

Read the extract below and then attempt the following questions.

Sailmaker by Alan Spence

1 BILLY: Hey. Remember when we were wee, we used to fight like cat an dog?

    DAVIE: Ah could beat ye an all!

    BILLY: Oh aye, ye were too fast for me. Quick on yer feet. The old one-two. Ma only chance was tae get ye in a bearhug.

5 DAVIE: Ah've still got the bruises!

    BILLY: Ah remember one time we were havin a right old barney, an da was tryin tae sleep – must've been on the nightshift. An he came runnin out the room in his shirt-tail an clattered the pair ae us!

    DAVIE: He was a tough auld customer right enough. Had tae be in these days.

10 BILLY: D'ye know he walked fae Campbeltown tae Glasgow tae get a start in the yards! Tellin ye, we don't know we're livin.

          Ah hear the boy's daein well at school.

    DAVIE: Oh aye. He's clever. He'll get on.

    BILLY: He'll get on a lot better if you screw the heid, right?

15 DAVIE: C'mon, Billy, ah dae ma best. It's just …

    BILLY: Ah know it's hard on yer own an that …

    DAVIE: Naw ye don't know. Naebody knows, unless they've been through it. (*Quieter*) Comin hame's the worst. The boy's oot playin. Hoose is empty. Gets on top of ye.

20   The other night there, ah got this queer feelin. Ah felt as if aw the furniture and everythin was *watching* me. Sounds daft, eh? Maybe ah'm goin aff ma heid!

    BILLY: Bound tae take a while tae get over it.

    DAVIE: If ah ever dae.

(*They cross to where ALEC is playing with yacht*)

    BILLY: (*To ALEC*) How ye doin wee yin? What's this ye've got? (*Picks up yacht*)

25 ALEC: Used tae be Jacky's.

    DAVIE: Ah'm gonnae fix it up, when ah've got the time.

    ALEC: Ye've been sayin that for weeks!

BILLY: Ah could paint it if ye like.

ALEC: Would ye?

30 BILLY: Aye, sure. Should come up really nice. Ah'll take it away wi me. Get it done this week.

ALEC: This week!

BILLY: Nae bother.

ALEC: What colours will ye make it?

BILLY: Ah think the hull has tae be white. Ah've got a nice white gloss at work. The keel ah
35 could dae in blue. Maybe put a wee blue rim round the edge here. An ah think ah've
got a light brown that would do just fine for the deck. That suit ye awright?

ALEC: Great!

BILLY: Ye won't even recognise it. It'll be like a brand new boat.

ALEC: It'll be dead real, eh?

40 BILLY: It'll be that real we can aw sail away in it!

DAVIE: Away tae Never Never Land!

BILLY: Right, ah'll be seein ye.

(*Takes yacht, exits*)

(*Alec follows him seeing him out, then comes back*)

45 ALEC: Uncle Billy's great isn't he.

1. Look at lines 1 to 5.

By referring to **one** example of language, explain what we learn about the relationship between the brothers Billy and Davie.

2

2. Look at lines 13 to 17.

By referring to **two** examples of language, show how the atmosphere of the scene changes when Billy says 'He'll get on a lot better if you screw the heid, right?'

4

3. Look at lines 16 to 21.

By referring to **two** examples of language, explain how the writer makes it clear that Davie is unhappy.

4

4. Look at lines 30 to 42.

By referring to **one** example of language, explain how the writer makes the model yacht seem important.

2

5. By referring to this extract and to elsewhere in the play, show how the writer presents the character of Davie.

8

OR

Text 3 – Drama

If you choose this text you may not attempt a question on Drama in Section 2.

Read the extract below and then attempt the following questions.

Tally's Blood by Ann Marie Di Mambro

In this extract, Lucia and Hughie are playing a game in the Ginger Store of the Pedrescis' shop.

1 LUCIA: Come on, come on, seven and five? He's not doing very well, is he boys and girls?

   HUGHIE: Seven and five?

   LUCIA: You heard.

5 *Pokes him with pointer.*

   HUGHIE: Seven ADD ON five you mean?

   LUCIA: You heard.

Pokes him with pointer.

Hughie tries to count on fingers, mouthing figures, gets to 'seven' then to 'ten'. Lucia makes him lose
10 *count: jabs him with her pointer.*

   LUCIA: Too long! I can't spend all day with one child. I've got all these other little children to see to as well, you know. Little SCOTTISH boys and girls. I think they deserve some of the teacher's time too. You should have done these sums last night, Franco. Why didn't you?

15 HUGHIE: Eh, well, I forgot.

   LUCIA: Oh, you forgot, did you? Do you hear that, boys and girls? Little Franco 'forgot'. Sure you weren't too busy serving the shop?

   HUGHIE: No, miss.

   LUCIA: Or maybe you don't have pencils in your house. Or maybe you don't have a
20 house. Have you got a house?

   HUGHIE: Yes, miss.

   LUCIA: No use telling fibs, now, is it, Franco? We all know you live in a shop. Now don't laugh, boys and girls. It's not Franco's fault he lives in a shop.

   HUGHIE: Twelve.

25 LUCIA: Oh, so there's twelve of you living there. My oh my! Not all in the same bed, I hope. Now stop laughing, boys and girls, it's not funny.

   HUGHIE: Seven and five is twelve.

LUCIA: Oh, you're too late now. I don't know what you're doing in this class in the first place. A little ruffian like you. A sleekit little, greasy little, smelly little ...

30 *It's gone too far. Hughie jumps up. Knocks away his ginger box.*

HUGHIE: I don't like this game.

LUCIA: Well, I don't like it either.

They are staring at each other: it is broken by Rosinella's screams.

ROSINELLA: (*Voice from offstage*) Lucia! Lucia!

35 *Rosinella, highly distraught, clutching a newspaper, in the back shop: Lucia and Hughie run to her: she thrusts the paper at them.*

ROSINELLA: Lucia, Lucia, what's it say? What's it say? Tell me what it says. (*Blessing herself*) Oh, Sant' Antonio, San Guiseppe. Oh no, don't tell me. Oh, Massimo, Massimo!

1. Look at lines 1 to 4.

   By referring to **two** examples, explain what impression is created of the characters of the children.

   4

2. Look at lines 11 to 29.

   By referring to **two** examples of language, explain how the writer makes Lucia's portrayal of the teacher seem cruel.

   4

3. Look at lines 31 to 36.

   By referring to **two** examples, explain how the writer makes Rosinella's entrance dramatic.

   4

4. By referring to this extract and to elsewhere in the play, show how the theme of racism is explored.

   8

Section 1 Part A Drama – Model Answers
Text 1 – *Yellow Moon*

1. The comical rhymes ('Double G'/'so hornee') of Lee's invented rap (1) communicate his humour and bravado (1). Lee is funny and full of life.

   The powerful rhythms in the rap ('Like Bambi's dad. I drive girls mad.') (1) suggest his energy and vibrant personality (1).

   The motif/symbol of the stag (1) enables Lee to create a persona for himself that makes him seem strong, handsome and capable (1).

   The stag represents a powerful and noble masculinity (1), which is ironic because Lee is poor and almost powerless (1).

   The idea of Lee becoming an American-style gangster pimp in Inverkeithing is so unlikely and exaggerated (1) it is ridiculous, but it is also endearing because he is making fun of himself (1).

2. The writer creates a contrast (1) to emphasise how Leila is a completely different character to Lee (1).

   Leila does not speak in the extract; we only read her internal thoughts (1). This shows she is introverted and thoughtful (1).

   Leila's thoughts and personality are revealed as interior monologue and come out here as questions (1) indicating her insecurity and uncertainty about herself (1): 'Did I make that happen?', 'Well did she?'

3. Using aggressive questions, Billy demands that Lee answers him ('Where's the ring?', 'Where is it?') (1) – this shows he is confrontational and controlling (1).

   Billy also gives Lee orders or commands ('Get up.', 'Get up and fight.') (1), demonstrating that he is aggressive (1).

4. The stage directions list (1) four aggressive actions that Billy carries out (1). (Billy punches Lee in the stomach. Billy pushes Lee. Billy pushes Lee again. Billy pushes Lee and this time Lee falls.)

   In comparison, Lee does not react (Lee stays down) (1). This shows that Billy is the aggressor and the instigator of violence, while Lee is passive at first (1).

5. Lee's comical rap about becoming a pimp is an overblown and exaggerated fantasy where he imagines himself as powerful and attractive. This is ironic, and is a contrast to the real Lee, who is in fact deeply insecure because of his uncertainty about his father's identity, his mother's depression and the fact that he has been bullied and traumatised by Billy. To escape the reality of his fragile masculinity, Lee imagines himself as a tough and attractive criminal.

Billy Logan is full of hate and is probably a misogynist at heart. If he really loved Lee's mother, Jenni, he would try to help Lee and be kind to him. Billy shows nothing but aggression towards Lee: 'You are a catastrophe, Lee Macalinden ... a fucking catastrophe'. Lee's stabbing of Billy is provoked by Billy's violence, and although in the eyes of the law Lee has committed a terrible crime, we feel that Billy deserves his fate. Billy's last thoughts as he is dying are despicable, hateful, sexist profanities.

Later in the play, when Lee and Leila's relationship becomes physical, Lee is confused and a little frightened. He thinks he should be forceful and aggressive, but he doesn't really want to be. This is shown in his stilted language and the way he contradicts himself: 'I want to push you down – just rough like I'm in charge – I'm going to push you down – I don't want to push you down'. Lee isn't sure how a man should behave. Leila, by contrast, takes control and instructs him calmly and gently 'Take off your clothes'.

When Lee eventually does get to know his father, he learns that his father is not a successful gangster, but a sad alcoholic who is nevertheless managing to make a small living on a Highland estate. Frank is a contradictory figure, who has lost out in life but still manages to show Lee and Leila how to live a more connected and satisfying life on the estate. Frank's masculinity is weak, and he has failed to be a father to Lee. As he says, 'this isn't a story, it's a fuck up'. Frank at least admits his inadequacies as a man when he acknowledges 'all of this is my fault' – he achieves some redemption for his weaknesses and his past mistakes.

So, the male figures of Billy and Frank are examples of weak men. But there may be hope for the future for Lee, who has a redeeming strength, charisma and humour, as well as Leila's love and wisdom to guide and inspire him.

- Comical rap about becoming a pimp (1) is an overblown and exaggerated fantasy where he imagines himself as powerful and attractive (1).

- This is ironic, and a contrast to the real Lee (1), who is insecure because of his uncertainty about his father's identity, his mother's depression and Billy's aggression (1).

- To escape the reality of his fragile masculinity (1), Lee imagines himself as a tough and attractive criminal (1).

- Billy Logan is full of hate and misogyny (1). If his love for Jenni was real, he would try to help Lee (1).

- Toxic masculinity. Billy shows aggression to Lee: 'You are a catastrophe, Lee Macalinden ... a fucking catastrophe' (1). Lee's stabbing of Billy is provoked by Billy's violence (1).

- Lee has committed a terrible crime, but we feel that Billy deserves his fate. Billy's masculinity is toxic (1) and his last thoughts as he is dying are hateful, sexist profanities (1).

- Commonality/elsewhere in the text: As Lee and Leila's relationship develops, this reveals Lee's confused ideas about masculinity in his language and the way he contradicts himself: 'I want to push you down – just rough like I'm in charge – I'm going to push you down – I don't want to push you down' (1). Lee isn't sure how a man should behave (1).

- Lee's father is not a successful gangster or a good masculine role model (1), but a sad alcoholic who makes a small living on a Highland estate (1).

- Frank's masculinity is weak and he has failed to be a father to Lee (1). As he says, 'this isn't a story, it's a fuck up' (1).

- Frank admits his inadequacies as a man when he acknowledges 'all of this is my fault' (1). He achieves some redemption for his weaknesses and his past mistakes (1).

TOP TIP

To help you to structure your final answer on prose or drama, you might choose to use words like **initially**, **later**, **eventually** and **finally**. These will help you to arrange your points in order.

Text 2 – *Sailmaker*

1. The dialogue reveals that Billy and Davie get on reasonably well together. Billy's appeal to Davie to 'Remember when we were wee, we used to fight like cat an dog?' (1) invites him to reminisce with his brother and gives us the impression that their fighting is now mostly in the past (1).

2. The mood is relaxed and friendly (1) at the beginning of the extract as they remember their childhood fights fondly: 'Ah could beat ye an all!' (1).

   The mood becomes unsettled and some tension creeps into the dialogue (1) when Billy says that Davie should 'screw the heid'. Davie seems annoyed with Billy for confronting him in this way (1).

3. Dialogue – Davie interrupts Billy abruptly with 'Naw ye don't know.'

   The stage direction '(*quieter*)' suggests that he realises he may have been slightly aggressive to begin with but has calmed down a little.

   Davie uses three short sentences with a similar rhythm in each to express the reasons for his unhappiness: 'The boy's oot playin. Hoose is empty. Gets on top of ye.'

4. In the extract, the yacht starts to become a symbol of fantasy and escapism (1) when Davie says they might sail off 'tae Never Never Land', maybe to escape their unhappy life (1). Although Billy has exciting plans to paint the model and restore it, the fact that he doesn't do this is also important – this shows that he has very little strength or determination left.

> The following mini-essay style answer is provided to help you think about the question and the wider text.
>
> The bullet-point version of the answer that follows is intended to help you create your own answer. It is highly recommended that you choose the bullet-point approach for this question type.

5. Davie has a difficult life. When the play begins, we learn that he has just lost his wife. He becomes a single parent to Alec. They are a working-class family, and the loss of industry in Glasgow has meant that things are very difficult for Davie; he has lost his job as a skilled tradesman – a sailmaker - and he has to take poorly paid jobs. I think he suffers from a loss of his dignity because he isn't doing anything that challenges him in his working life.

Davie turns to alcohol ('You've been drinkin. Ah can smell it.') and gambles his money in the hope of a big win which could make life better for him. Alec does not like Davie drinking, and Billy is against his betting and his drinking ('Ye bettin too heavy? Is that it?'). This causes conflict between Davie and his son, and between Davie and his brother, hence Billy suggesting in the extract that Davie should 'screw the heid'.

It may be that Davie feels that he is a failure in comparison to his younger brother, who seems to be in control of his life and is idolised by Alec ('Billy's great'), and maybe he feels patronised by his brother's advice. Davie certainly doesn't seem to be as tough as his father, who walked from Campbeltown to Glasgow to find a job. Davie may have been good at boxing when he was younger but was obviously not good enough to become professional. He perhaps isn't the best father he could be to Alec, but he still encourages him in his schoolwork and his religion, and he sometimes plays at boxing with him for fun. All in all, Davie is not a bad father to Alec, but he has some shortcomings which we might say are not his own fault.

Here is the example answer as bullet-points which is the recommended method.

- Davie becomes a single parent to Alec (1), so audience has sympathy for him (1).
- Elsewhere in the play (commonality) we learn Davie has lost his job as a skilled tradesman (1) – a sailmaker – and has to take poorly paid jobs and suffers a loss of dignity (1).
- Davie turns to alcohol ('You've been drinkin. Ah can smell it.') and gambles his money (1) in the false hope of a big win which could make life better for him (1).
- Alec does not like Davie drinking, and Billy is against his betting and his drinking (1) – 'Ye bettin too heavy? Is that it?' (1).
- This causes conflict between Davie and his son, and between Davie and his brother (1), hence Billy suggesting in the extract that Davie should 'screw the heid' (1).
- Davie may feel that he is a failure in comparison to his younger brother, who seems to be in control of his life and is idolised by Alec ('Billy's great') (1), and maybe he feels patronised by his brother's advice (1).
- Davie certainly doesn't seem to be as tough as his father (1), who walked from Campbeltown to Glasgow to find a job (1).
- Davie may have been good at boxing when he was younger but was obviously not good enough to become professional, again showing his shortcomings (1).
- He perhaps isn't the best father he could be to Alec, but he still encourages him in his schoolwork and his religion (1), and he sometimes plays at boxing with him for fun (1).

Text 3 – *Tally's Blood*

1. Lucia plays the teacher – she is bossy and likes to be in charge. Lucia is the dominant one of the two children (1). For example, she is pressurising Hughie for an answer: 'Come on, come on, seven and five?' (1).

   Hughie, on the other hand, seems happy to do as he is told (1). He plays along and is more compliant, asking questions of Lucia – 'Seven and five?' (1)

2. Language:

   She talks to an imaginary class – 'boys and girls' (1) – as if to humiliate him in front of others (1).

   She makes out that his family are poor (1). She pretends his answer to the sum is the number of children who live together in his overcrowded shop (1).

   She uses unkind adjectives 'sleekit', 'greasy' and 'smelly' (1) to describe him (1). 'Sleekit' is Scots for sly and untrustworthy. These words build to a climax in the scene.

   Stage directions:

   She 'pokes' him with the pointer, and then 'jabs' him (1). These directions make it seem like it would be violent and painful (1).

3. The children are staring at each other in a confrontation (1). This is interrupted by Rosinella's voice, so this is dramatic to start with (1).

   Rosinella is screaming (1) – this adds to the drama (1).

   She 'thrusts' the newspaper at Lucia to get her to read it (1) – this suggests a very powerful and dramatic movement (1).

   She asks frantic questions, 'blesses herself' and prays to the saints – her religion is important to her at times of stress (1). This also adds to the drama (1).

> The following mini-essay style answer is provided to help you think about the question and the wider text.
>
> The bullet-point version of the answer that follows is intended to help you create your own answer. It is highly recommended that you choose the bullet-point approach for this question type.

4. When she is playing the teacher, Lucia refers to some racist stereotypes of Italians and shows what some of the Scots think about Italians. She suggests that they are dirty ('greasy') and that they are not trustworthy ('sleekit'). She also suggests that they are poor and have to live in shops rather than houses. When she says 'I've got

all these other little children to see to as well, you know. Little SCOTTISH boys and girls', this makes the audience think that the teacher resents having Italian children in her class and would rather teach Scottish children. She makes out that the Italian boy, Franco, is stupid.

In other parts of the play, we see racism towards the Italians when, at the start of the war, an angry mob vandalises Massimo's shop, and when Massimo is imprisoned and taken away. Massimo is a hardworking, peaceful, loving, kind man, who wouldn't hurt anyone – but he is treated terribly. He is separated from his elderly father, and then his father dies.

There is also racism from the Italians towards the Scots. Rosinella is determined that Lucia will marry an Italian man and is horrified at the idea of Lucia marrying Hughie. She thinks that Scottish boys are not good enough for her niece. Using harsh, colloquial language, she calls Hughie a 'jumped up wee piece of nothing', when actually he is a kind and hardworking boy.

Rosinella is also unkind to Hughie's sister, Bridget, and thinks she is not good enough for Franco, Massimo's brother. The play is very ironic when Rosinella discovers that Bridget was pregnant to Franco but has terminated the pregnancy. If Rosinella hadn't been racist towards Bridget, Bridget and Franco might have married and the baby might have been born. To conclude, racism causes a great deal of hurt and unhappiness in this play.

Here is the example answer as bullet-points which is the recommended method.

- Lucia refers to some racist stereotypes and shows what some of the Scots think about Italians (1). Suggests that they are dirty ('greasy'), and that they are not trustworthy ('sleekit') (1).
- Lucia suggests that they are poor (1) and must live in shops rather than houses (1).
- Says 'I've got ... Little SCOTTISH boys and girls' (1) – shows she resents having Italian children (1).
- She implies (1) the Italian boy, Franco, is stupid (1).
- Elsewhere (commonality), racism (1) towards the Italians as mob vandalises Massimo's shop (1).
- Racism (1) when Massimo is unjustly imprisoned (1).
- Massimo is a hardworking, peaceful, loving, kind man (1) but he is treated terribly because of racism (1).
- Further racism (1) when Massimo is separated from his elderly father, and then his father dies (1).

- Racism from the Italians towards the Scots. Rosinella is determined that Lucia will marry an Italian man and is horrified at the idea of Lucia marrying Hughie (1), revealing her racism (1).
- Rosinella is racist, thinking Scottish boys are not good enough for her niece (1). Harsh, colloquial language, calling Hughie a 'jumped up wee piece of nothing'. (1)
- Rosinella is racist towards Hughie's sister (1) and thinks she is not good enough for Franco, Massimo's brother (1).
- Tragic and ironic (1) when Rosinella discovers that Bridget was pregnant to Franco but has terminated the pregnancy (1).

Text 1 - Prose

If you choose this text you may not attempt a question on Prose in Section 2.

Read the extract below and then attempt the following questions.

The Strange Case of Dr Jekyll and Mr Hyde by Robert Louis Stevenson

In this extract, the lawyer, Mr Utterson, interrupts and confronts Mr Hyde as he is returning to the laboratory.

1 'And now,' said the other, 'how did you know me?'

'By description,' was the reply.

'Whose description?'

'We have common friends,' said Mr Utterson.

5 'Common friends?' echoed Mr Hyde, a little hoarsely. 'Who are they?'

'Jekyll, for instance,' said the lawyer.

'He never told you,' cried Mr Hyde, with a flush of anger. 'I did not think you would have lied.'

'Come,' said Mr Utterson, 'that is not fitting language.'

The other snarled aloud into a savage laugh, and the next moment, with extraordinary
10 quickness, he had unlocked the door and disappeared into the house.

The lawyer stood awhile when Mr Hyde had left him, the picture of disquietude. Then he
began slowly to mount the street, pausing every step or two and putting his hand to his
brow like a man in mental perplexity. The problem he was thus debating as he walked, was
one of a class that was rarely solved. Mr Hyde was pale and dwarfish, he gave an impression
15 of deformity without any nameable malformation, he had a displeasing smile, he had borne
himself to the lawyer with a sort of murderous mixture of timidity and boldness, and he spoke
with a husky, whispering, and somewhat broken voice; all these were points against him,
but not all of these together could explain the hitherto unknown disgust, loathing and fear
with which Mr Utterson regarded him. 'There must be something else,' said the perplexed
20 gentleman. 'There is something more, if I could find a name for it. God bless me, the man
seems hardly human! Something troglodytic, shall we say? or can it be the old story of Dr Fell?
or is it the mere radiance of a foul soul that thus transpires through, and transfigures, its clay
continent? The last, I think; for O my poor old Harry Jekyll, if ever I read Satan's signature on a
face, it is on that of your new friend.'

25 Round the corner from the bystreet, there was a square of ancient, handsome houses, now
for the most part decayed from their high estate and let in flats and chambers to all sorts
and conditions of men: map engravers, architects, shady lawyers, and the agents of obscure

enterprises. One house, however, second from the corner, was still occupied entire, and at the door of this, which wore a great air of wealth and comfort, though it was now plunged in darkness except for the fan light, Mr Utterson stopped and knocked. A well-dressed, elderly servant opened the door.

'Is Dr Jekyll at home, Poole?' asked the lawyer.

'I will see, Mr Utterson,' said Poole, admitting the visitor as he spoke, into a large, low-roofed, comfortable room, paved with flags, warmed (after the fashion of a country house) by a bright, open fire, and furnished with costly cabinets of oak. 'Will you wait here by the fire, sir, or shall I give you a light in the dining room?'

1. Look at lines 5 to 10.

   Referring to **two** examples of language, show how the character of Mr Hyde is revealed in the extract.

   4

2. Look at lines 11 to 24.

   Referring to **two** examples of language, show how the writer reveals Mr Utterson's state of mind.

   4

3. Look at lines 25 to 31.

   Referring to **two** examples of language, show what impressions the writer creates of Dr Jekyll's house.

   4

4. By referring to this extract and to elsewhere in the novel, show how the writer explores the theme of deception.

   8

Text 2 – Prose

If you choose this text you may not attempt a question on Prose in Section 2.

Read the extract below and then attempt the following questions.

Duck Feet by Ely Percy

In this extract from the chapter 'Social Dancing', Kirsty and some of her classmates are sitting at the side of the hall while the rest of the class are dancing. The teacher confronts Charlene.

1   An what's your excuse for not takin part today Miss Clark. It isnae an excuse, said Charlene,
Ah've got a sair stomach. Have you brought a note, he said. How could ah bring a note, sir, she
said, Ah cannae predict if ah'm gaunnae be no well. Well, it seems to me, said Mister Anderson,
That this is a re-occurrin illness and if it persists ah'll have to ask you to bring a letter from your
5   doctor. OK. Naw, said Charlene. I beg your pardon, said Mister Anderson. It's ma time ae the
month, she said, O.kaay. Mister Anderson walked away shakin his heid. Dick, said Charlene,
under her breath, then she looked at me fur confirmation that he wis. Aye well that's him
shattered, Charlene said tae Kelly Marie, How did you no say yi had yir period. Kelly Marie
shrugged an then showed aff wan haun wi Tipex coatet fingernails an wee green pictures;
10   then she turnt roon tae Harpreet an said, Heh hingmy – whit's that religious lassie's name again
– Harpreach or whatever your name is, how come he didnae pull you up. Sorry, said Harpreet,
she looked up fae the textbook she wis readin. How you no daein it, said Kelly Marie. Oh, said
Harpreet, It's—

Harpreet didnae get the chance tae answer though cause Charlene jamp in an spoke ower the
15   top ae her. Sa against your religion tae dae social dancin int it, she said, lookin pure pleased wi
hersel. Actually no, said Harpreet, It's because – Aye it is, said Charlene, Don't gies it – We went
a trip tae the mosque when we wur in primary so ah know thir's loadsa shit your wans arenae
allowed tae dae. Harpreet giggult. Ah'm not a Muslim, she said, But it's OK ah'm not offended
– lotsa folk get us muddled up. Charlene pult a face. Ma parents jist don't want me doin social
20   dancin, she said, Because in Punjabi culture it's seen as taboo fur boys an girls tae dance
together – although obviously not everyone upholds that tradition which is why—

Och who gives a shit, said Charlene, Everythin else is against your bliddy religion!

Ah wis proper gobsmacked by that. So wis Harpreet ah think. Ah thought whit Harpreet wis
sayin wis dead interesting, but of course ah never got tae hear the rest ae the conversation.
25   Harpreet's dead nice anaw, and she's been a much better pal tae me than Charlene has lately.
Ah don't know whit Charlene's problem is but nearly everything that comes oot her mooth
these days is dead sarky.

There wis a pure awkward silence after that. Then Kelly Marie, who had jist finished Tipexin her
other haun hit oot we, Heh whit religion are you anyway. Hapreet said, Ah'm a Sikh. Seek, said
30   Kelly Marie, Yi don't look no well tae me, and then her an Charlene startet sniggern. Charlene
said, Next time we get tolt tae dae Social Dancin ah'm gaunnae say ah cannae cause it's against
ma religion.

1. Look at lines 1 to 13.

Referring to **two** examples of language, show how the author creates humour.

4

2. Referring to **two** examples of language, show how the author reveals the character of Charlene in the extract.

4

3. Referring to **two** examples of language, show how the author reveals the character of Harpreet in the extract.

4

4. Show how the author explores the theme of friendship in this extract and elsewhere in 'Part Wan' of the novel.

8

Text 3 – Prose

If you choose this text you may not attempt a question on Prose in Section 2.

Read the extract below and then attempt the following questions.

From *All That Glisters* by Anne Donovan

1 *Would you like to use the glitter pens?*

And she pulled oot the pack fae her bag.

Ah'd never seen them afore. When ah wis in Primary Four the teacher gied us tubes of glitter but it wis quite messy. Hauf the stuff ended up on the flair and it wis hard tae make sure you
5 got the glue in the right places. But these pens were different cos the glue wis mixed in wi the glitter so you could jist draw with them. It wis pure brilliant, so it wis. There wis four colours, rid, green, gold and silver, and it took a wee while tae get the hang of it. You had tae be careful when you squeezed the tube so's you didnae get a big blob appearin at wanst, but efter a few goes ah wis up an runnin.

10 And when ah'd finished somethin amazin hud happened. Ah cannae explain whit it wis but the glitter jist brought everythin tae life, gleamin and glisterin agin the flat cardboard. It wis like the difference between a Christmas tree skinklin wi fairy lights and wan lyin deid and daurk in a corner.

Ma daddy wis dead chuffed. He pit the card on the bedside table and smiled.

15 *Fair brightens up this room, hen.*

It's good tae find sumpn that cheers him up even a wee bit because ma daddy's really sick. He's had a cough for as long as ah can remember, and he husny worked for years, but these past three months he cannae even get oot his bed. Ah hear him coughin in the night sometimes and it's different fae the way he used tae cough, comes fae deeper inside him somehow, seems
20 tae rack his hale body fae inside oot. When ah come in fae school ah go and sit wi him and tell him aboot whit's happened that day, but hauf the time he looks away fae me and stares at a patch on the downie cover where there's a coffee stain that ma ma cannae wash oot. He used tae work strippin oot buildins and he wis breathin in stour aw day, sometimes it wis that bad he'd come hame wi his hair and his claes clartit wi it. He used tae kid on he wis a ghost and
25 walk in the hoose wi his airms stretched oot afore him and ah'd rin and hide unner the stair, watchin him walk by wi the faint powdery whiteness floatin roon his heid.

He never knew there wis asbestos in the dust, never knew a thing aboot it then, nane o them did. Noo he's an expert on it, read up aw these books tae try and unnerstaun it fur the compensation case. Before he got really sick he used tae talk aboot it sometimes.

30 *You see, hen, the word asbestos comes fae a Greek word that means indestructible. That's how they use it fur fireproofin – the fire cannae destroy it.*

You mean if you wore an asbestos suit you could walk through fire and it widnae hurt you?

Aye. In the aulden days they used tae bury royals in it. They cried it the funeral dress of kings.

Questions

1. Look at lines 1 to 9.

   By referring to **one** example of language, explain how the writer creates a clear impression of the story's narrator.

   2

2. Look at lines 10 to 13.

   By referring to **two** examples of language, show how the writer makes it clear that the girl feels joy and excitement.

   4

3. Look at lines 16 to 26.

   By referring to **two** examples of language, show how the writer creates a sense of sadness.

   4

4. Look at lines 27 to 33.

   By referring to **one** example of language, explain what these lines reveal about the narrator's father.

   2

5. Referring to *All That Glisters* and to at least **one** other story, show how Donovan explores the theme of childhood.

   8

Text 4 – Prose

If you choose this text you may not attempt a question on Prose in Section 2.

Read the extract below and then attempt the following questions.

From *Death in a Nut*, as told by Duncan Williamson

1   Jack used tae always get up early in the mornin an make a cup o tea, he always gev his mother
a cup o tea in bed every mornin. An one particular mornin he rose early because he want't tae
catch the in-comin tide tae see what it wad bring in fir him. He brought a cup o tea into his
mother in her own little bed in a little room, it wis only a two-room little cottage they had.

5   He says, 'Mother, I've brought you a cup o tea.'

She says, 'Son, I don't want any tea.'

'Mother,' he says, 'why? What's wrong, are you not feelin—'

She says, 'Son, I'm not feelin very well this morning, I'm not feelin very well. I don't think I cuid
even drink a cup o tea if ye gev it to me.'

10   'Oh, Mother,' he says, 'try an take a wee sip,' an he leaned over the bed, held the cup to his
mother's mooth an tried to get her ...

She took two–three sips, 'That's enough, laddie,' she says, 'I don't feel very well.'

He says, 'What's wrong with you, Mother? Are you in pain or somethin?'

'Well, so an no so, Jack, I dinnae ken what's wrong wi me,' she says. 'I'm an ill woman, Jack, an
15   ye're a young man an I cannae go on for ever.'

'But, Mother,' he says, 'you cannae dee an leave me masel! What am I gaunnae dae? I've nae
freends, nae naebody in this worl but you, Mother! Ye cannae dee an lea me!'

'Well,' she says, 'Jack, I think I'm no long fir this worl. In fact, I think he'll be comin fir me some o
these days ... soon.'

20   'Wha, Mother, ye talking about "comin fir me"?'

She says, 'Jack, ye ken wha he is, Jack. Between me an you, we dinna share nae secrets –

I'm an auld woman an I'm gaunna dee – Death's gaunna come fir me, Jack, I can see it in ma
mind.'

'Oh, Mother, no, Mother,' he says, an he held her hand.

25   'But,' she says, 'never mind, laddie, ye'll manage to take care o yirsel. Yir mother hes saved a
few shillins fir ye an I'm sure some day ye'll meet a nice wee wife when I'm gone, ye'll prob'ly
get on in the world.'

'No, Mother,' he says, 'I cuidna get on withoot you.'

She says, 'Laddie, leave me an I'll try an get a wee sleep.'

30 Bi this time it was daylight as the sun begint tae get up an Jack walkit up along the shoreway jist in the grey-dark in the mornin, gettin clear. It must hae been about half-past eight–nine o'clock (in the wintertime it took a long while tae get clear in the mornins) when the tide was comin in.

Jack walked along the shoreway an lo an behold, the first thing he seen comin a-walkin the
35 shoreway was an auld man with a long grey beard, skinny legs and a ragged coat o'er his back an a scythe on his back. His two eyes were sunk inta his heid, sunk back intae his skull, an he wis the most uglies'-luikin creature that Jack ever seen in his life. But he had on his back *a brand new scythe* an hit was shinin in the light fae the mornin.

1. Look at lines 1 to 4.

   By referring to **one** example of language, explain how the storyteller reveals that Jack and his mother live a simple life without much wealth.

   2

2. Look at lines 5 to 13.

   By referring to **one** example of language, explain how the storyteller reveals the relationship between Jack and his mother.

   2

3. Look at lines 16 to 17.

   Referring to **two** features of language, show how the storyteller reveals Jack's distress when his mother says she is dying.

   4

4. Look at lines 34 to 38.

   Referring to **two** features of language, show how the storyteller creates a sinister impression of the 'auld man'.

   4

5. By referring to *Death in a Nut* and to **one** other Scottish short story from the list, show how the writers explore the theme of the supernatural.

   8

Section 1 Part B Prose – Model answers

Text 1 – *The Strange Case of Dr Jekyll and Mr Hyde*

1. The choice of the word 'snarled' (1) suggests Hyde sounded aggressive and animal-like (1).

   His laugh is described using the adjective 'savage' (1). 'Savage' is the opposite of civilized and suggests he may be dangerous or even violent (1).

2. The sentence beginning 'Mr Hyde was pale ...' is exceptionally long, listing repulsive aspects of Mr Hyde and extending the description of Mr Utterson's thoughts with the use of a semi-colon (1). This reflects the range and speed of the thoughts passing through Mr Utterson's mind (1).

   An exclamation ('... the man seems hardly human!') and a series of three questions (1) show that he is nervously excited and deeply perplexed (1).

3. The house 'wore a great air of wealth and comfort' (1). The choice of words makes the house seem large, spacious and opulent (1).

   But the lighting may symbolise something sinister (1): 'it was now plunged in darkness' (1). The house seems both homely and disturbing.

The following mini-essay style answer is provided to help you think about the question and the wider text.

The bullet-point version of the answer that follows is intended to help you create your own answer. It is highly recommended that you choose the bullet-point approach for this question type.

---

4. Deception is a very important idea in this novel.

   In the extract, Mr Hyde is shown as the rough, uncouth, dangerous alter ego of the pleasant and mannerly Dr Jekyll. He is angry, speaks 'hoarsely' and is full of an unsettling energy. His name – 'Hyde' – is a pun on the word 'hide' and suggests that Dr Jekyll would prefer to conceal this wicked aspect of himself. The good Dr Jekyll represents science, rationality and reason, while Mr Hyde represents the concealed, subconscious evil desires and violent urges that can be part of human nature.

   Dr Jekyll's house itself seems to suggest a deceptive double meaning. In the extract it was once a grand and beautiful house, but now the other houses around it have been divided up and some are inhabited by dubious and immoral people like 'shady lawyers' and the 'agents of obscure enterprises'. The front of the house that can be seen on the square is respectable and looks good, while the laboratory at the back is windowless and sinister, symbolising the concealed evil that goes on there.

Later in the story, Dr Jekyll himself remarks that 'man is not truly one, but truly two', hinting that humanity cannot escape from the terrible Mr Hyde lurking beneath the surface. Jekyll talks openly of 'deception' and 'duplicity'. As the story progresses towards its end, Mr Hyde begins to overcome Dr Jekyll. Jekyll describes his two selves in a striking metaphor as 'polar twins continually struggling'. This makes us think that there is no real division between good and evil, but that human beings must work to keep themselves in check, to remain respectable and to do good.

> Here is the example answer as bullet-points which is the recommended method.

- Hyde is the rough, uncouth, dangerous alter ego (1) of pleasant, mannerly Dr Jekyll (1).
- Hyde is angry, speaks 'hoarsely' (1) and is full of unsettling energy (1).
- Name – 'Hyde' – is a pun (1) and suggests that Dr Jekyll would prefer to conceal this aspect of himself (1).
- Good Dr Jekyll represents science, rationality and reason (1); Hyde represents concealed, subconscious evil desires and violent urges (1).
- Dr Jekyll's house suggests a deceptive double meaning (1). Once grand and beautiful, now the neighbouring houses are inhabited by dubious and immoral 'shady lawyers' and the 'agents of obscure enterprises' (1).
- The front on the square looks good; the laboratory at the back is windowless and sinister (1), symbolising concealed evil (1).
- Later (commonality), Dr Jekyll remarks that 'man is not truly one, but truly two' (1), hinting humanity cannot escape from what lurks beneath the surface (1).
- Jekyll talks openly and directly (1) of 'deception' and 'duplicity' (1).
- Towards the end, Mr Hyde begins to overcome Dr Jekyll (1), showing evil may prevail (1).
- Jekyll uses a striking metaphor as 'polar twins continually struggling' (1), suggesting there may be no real division between good and evil (1), but that human beings must work to keep themselves in check, to remain respectable, and to do good.

Text 2 - *Duck Feet*

1. The author uses different, contrasting tones to create humour (1). So, the teacher speaks in formal English using phrases like 'if it persists' and 'I beg your pardon' while Charlene answers informally in her natural Scots language with 'Naw' and 'It's ma time ae the month' (1).

   Kelly Marie's language is very direct, and she is downright rude (1). She doesn't even bother to try to get Harpreet's name right: 'Heh hingmy – whit's that religious lassie's name again – Harpreach or whatever ...' (1).

   Harpreet, by comparison, is polite and happy to be studying (1): 'Sorry, said Harpreet, she looked up fae the textbook she wis readin.' (1) The contrast between the characters' language and attitudes creates humour.

2. Charlene seems very confident (1) in the way she talks to the teacher, challenging him directly by saying 'O.kaay', and calling him 'Dick' to Kirsty (1). Charlene seems arrogant (1) when she continually interrupts Harpreet without waiting to hear Harpreet's answers to her questions (1). Charlene uses rude and dismissive words like 'shit' and 'your bliddy religion!' (1), making her seem aggressive and intimidating (1).

3. The dialogue shows that Harpreet is calm and polite when other people pressurise (1) her – 'it's OK ah'm not offended' (1). Her choice of words shows she is articulate and has a wide vocabulary (1) – 'in Punjabi culture it's seen as taboo fur boys an girls tae dance together' (1). Harpreet seems to be a quiet, deep thinker (1) but she is also confident (1).

> The following mini-essay style answer is provided to help you think about the question and the wider text.
>
> The bullet-point version of the answer that follows is intended to help you create your own answer. It is highly recommended that you choose the bullet-point approach for this question type.

4. The extract shows some of the early stages of Kirsty's friendships with Charlene and Harpreet. Charlene is lively, funny and rude. Harpreet is thoughtful, quiet and deep. The title of this chapter – 'Social Dancing' – can be taken literally as the characters are learning to dance in PE, but the idea of 'social dancing' may also be a metaphor for them working out their relationships and how to get on with one another.

   As the story goes on, Kirsty remains friends with Charlene, even though Charlene is described by Kirsty's Mum as a 'user' and is often unkind to Kirsty, borrowing money from her and not paying it back, or making fun of Kirsty because Kirsty's family are in poverty. Kirsty thinks deeply about things, and is compassionate, understanding that Charlene's unkindness stems from her unhappiness and insecurities about her own family. Kirsty is a loyal, forgiving and understanding friend to Charlene, and sticks by her throughout the story, visiting her later when she is hospitalised with anorexia.

As the story progresses, Kirsty also finds she has a lot in common with Harpreet, and she is kind to Harpreet and understands their cultural differences. When Harpreet and her family move to England, Kirsty is genuinely upset and, as readers, we feel her sense of sadness and loss.

Here is the example answer as bullet-points which is the recommended method.

- Contrast: Charlene is lively, funny and rude (1); Harpreet is thoughtful, quiet and deep (1).
- Title of chapter – 'Social Dancing' – literally as characters are learning to dance in PE (1), but idea of 'social dancing' can also be metaphor for them working out relationships to one another (1).
- As the story goes on (commonality), Kirsty remains friends with Charlene (1), even though Charlene is described by Kirsty's Mum as a 'user' (1).
- Charlene is unkind (1) to Kirsty, borrowing money from her and not paying it back (1) or making fun of Kirsty because Kirsty's family are in poverty (1).
- Kirsty thinks deeply about things and is compassionate (1), understanding that Charlene's unkindness stems from her unhappiness and insecurities about her own family (1).
- Kirsty is a loyal, forgiving and understanding friend to Charlene (1), and sticks by her throughout, visiting her when she is hospitalised with anorexia (1).
- As the novel progresses, Kirsty discovers she has a lot in common with Harpreet (1), and she is kind to Harpreet and understands their cultural differences (1).
- When Harpreet and her family move to England (1), Kirsty is genuinely upset and we feel her sense of sadness and loss (1).

Candidate question

Is it OK to refer to the title of the chapter, poem or text you are writing about in the Scottish text section?

A Yes, it is. The title is absolutely part of the text, and if you want to mention it or analyse it – as in the example answer here on the chapter 'Social Dancing' – you certainly can.

Text 3 – *All That Glisters*

1. Reminiscing about 'Primary Four' (1) suggests the narrator of the story may still be a young girl at primary school (1).

    The narrator is excited about craft and colour (1) and uses the words 'pure brilliant' to show her enthusiasm (1).

    The narrator uses Scots language and phrases (1) such as 'Ah'd never seen them afore' (1).

2. Use of alliteration in 'gleamin and glisterin' (1) emphasises the moving light (1).

    Use of present participles (1) gives the impression that it is happening right now: 'gleamin and glisterin' (1).

    The simile of the Christmas tree with lights (1) creates a happy, joyous image (1).

    The choice of the word 'skinklin' (1) gives the sense of energy and movement (1).

3. Use of first-person narrator (1) makes it seem personal and poignant (1): 'ma daddy's really sick'.

    Choice of the word 'Daddy' (1) makes her sound like a young girl (1).

    Description of her father's cough is harsh, harrowing (1): 'seems tae rack his hale body fae inside oot' (1).

    Word choice of 'rack' (1) has harsh consonant sounds, sounds painful, suggests torture (1).

    Use of Glaswegian/Scots language and words (1) makes the description seem believable and convincing, gives the narrator a realistic, poignant voice: 'he cannae even get oot his bed' (1).

    The comparison of her father to a ghost 'wi the faint powdery whiteness floatin roon his heid' (1) seems ominous and sinister and may hint at the fact that he is about to die (1).

4. As well as having been a working man (1), the girl's father has studied hard – 'read up aw these books' (1).

    He is interested in language and history, and discusses etymology (1) – 'asbestos comes fae a Greek word' (1).

5. *All That Glisters* is a tender and sad story about a very difficult childhood experience. The narrator is a young girl, probably at primary school, who is close to her father. As the extract shows, she goes to talk to him daily about what has been going on at school.

Donovan writes very convincingly from a child's point of view in this story, using Scots language to create a realistic Glasgow voice for the girl: 'ma daddy says stealin is stealin'. When her dad eventually dies, the emotion is powerful but shown simply through action and very straightforward language: 'We sat for a long time, no speakin, just haudin hands'.

The narrator of *All That Glisters* is shown to be a very strong character. When her auntie forbids her to wear red at her dad's funeral, she rebels and covers her hair and face with glitter, thinking happily that her dad would have liked it: 'Aye, hen, subtle.'

Another story that looks at serious themes from the point of view of a child is *Hieroglyphics*. The narrator in this story is also a young schoolgirl, but in this story the focus is on the barriers to the girl's learning, and the fact that she is severely dyslexic.

Using her natural voice, Mary, the narrator, describes her learning need: 'how come flerr wisnae the same as merry and sterr wis different again and ma heid wis nippin wae coff and laff and though and bow …'. The story uses humour to show how pointless some of the learning seems to be in Mary's school, pointing out ironically that the collective nouns the class are learning would only be useful 'if Drumchapel ever got overrun by lions'.

Mary encounters one teacher – Mr Kelly – who is particularly unkind to her, ridiculing her work: 'What's this supposed to be – hieroglyphics?'. The story deals with the bullying, sarcasm and discrimination that Mary has to endure from this teacher, who is shown to be a snob, and doesn't understand her dyslexia or her intelligence. I find it particularly sad when Mary describes her own writing in a simile as 'a bit like wee scarab beetles scurryin aboot the page'.

Eventually, however, Mary takes a stand and completes what is supposed to be a written assignment using her own drawings or 'hieroglyphics', owning the insult the teacher has cast at her, and taking her own control of the situation, describing how she 'pit ma story right on tap ae the pile and planted the whole lot doon in the centre of his desk'. Although *Hieroglyphics* has an ambiguous ending, we are left feeling the narrator has moved on from her childhood insecurities and taken control of her own future.

- Convincingly told from a child's point of view (1), uses Scots language to create a realistic Glasgow voice: 'ma daddy says stealin is stealin' (1).
- Emotion is powerful but shown through action and very straightforward language (1): 'We sat for a long time, no speakin, just haudin hands' (1).
- Narrator of *All That Glisters* is a very strong character (1). Auntie forbids her to wear red at funeral, but she rebels and covers her hair and face with glitter, thinking her dad would have liked it: 'Aye, hen, subtle.' (1)
- Another story that looks at serious themes from the point of view of a child is *Hieroglyphics* (2 – commonality).
- Narrator in this story is also a young schoolgirl (1) but story focuses on barriers to the girl's learning and fact that she is severely dyslexic (1).
- Mary, the narrator, describes her learning need in the first person (1): 'how come flerr wisnae the same as merry …' (1).
- Story uses humour to show how pointless some of the learning seems to be, showing ironically (1) that the collective nouns the class are learning would only be useful 'if Drumchapel ever got overrun by lions' (1).
- One teacher, Mr Kelly, is particularly unkind to her, ridiculing her work: 'What's this supposed to be – hieroglyphics?' (1) – story deals with the bullying, sarcasm and discrimination (1).
- Teacher is a snob (1) and doesn't understand Mary's dyslexia or her intelligence (1).
- Mary describes her own writing in a simile as 'a bit like wee scarab beetles scurryin aboot the page' (1), suggesting untidy handwriting (1).
- Mary takes a stand and completes a written assignment using her own drawings or 'hieroglyphics' (1), owning the teacher's insult and taking control of the situation (1).
- Describes how she 'pit ma story right on tap ae the pile' (1). *Hieroglyphics* has an ambiguous ending, but we feel narrator has moved on from her childhood insecurities, taken control of her own future (1).

Text 4 – *Death in a Nut*

1. Jack beachcombs or scavenges for what he can find along the shore (1) – this suggests they don't have much money (1).

   His mother's bed and her room are both 'small' and the cottage they live in only has two rooms (1), again suggesting they are poor (1).

2. Jack brings his mother tea and helps and encourages her to drink it (1). He is her caregiver. He asks her questions about her wellbeing: 'What's wrong with you...?' and 'Are you in pain...?' (1). He is a kindly and concerned son (1).

3. Jack's distress is shown by his use of commands and exclamations (1): 'You cannae dee and leave me masel!' (1).

   He also uses repetition to show his distress (1) – 'nae freends, nae naebody...!' (1)
   He asks a question (1), showing his fear for the future, 'What am I gaunnae dae?' (1).

4. The 'auld man' is a personification of Death (1). He looks sickly, poor and repulsive, with thin legs and a 'ragged coat' (1). The references to his sunken eyes and his skull suggest decay and death (1). His 'brand new' scythe contrasts (1) with his tired, old, tattered appearance (1), and seems particularly sinister as it gleams in the morning light, ready to be used (1).

> The following mini-essay style answer is provided to help you think about the question and the wider text.
>
> The bullet-point version of the answer that follows is intended to help you create your own answer. It is highly recommended that you choose the bullet-point approach for this question type.

5. *Death in a Nut* is a traditional Scottish folk tale. In the extract, Jack dreads the arrival of Death and rails against him. As the story progresses, Jack beats Death temporarily, banishing him to the sea in a nutshell. Eventually, though, Jack comes to understand that death is a natural and necessary part of life, when Death tells him, 'Without me, there is no life'. When Jack releases Death, he agrees to spare Jack's mother for a time, so the supernatural element is not all bad in this story.

   In contrast, *Things My Wife and I Found Hidden in Our House* by Kirsty Logan is a modern supernatural tale. The supernatural element is a deeply sinister and malevolent kelpie, or water spirit. The narrator, Rain, imagines the items left in their new home are sweet and meant to wish them well. When Rain discovers the pearls on top of the wardrobe and puts them on, she says they are 'as long as a bridle'. The simile reminds us of the supernatural connection to kelpies and horses, and the pearls seem to enhance the women's passion and love for each other.

But the story becomes progressively more and more sinister when Alice's hand is burned by a weird copper horse, and Rain is nearly drowned in the bath by the kelpie. The end of the story is particularly sinister and ambiguous. Although the women try to exorcise the kelpie by throwing the gifts/items into the sea, and Rain begins to hope that 'women's love was stronger than women's hate', when they come home there is horsehair wrapped around their door handle, suggesting the evil haunting may continue.

> Here is the example answer as bullet-points which is the recommended method.

- In the extract, Jack dreads arrival of Death (1) and rails against him (1).
- Later, Jack beats Death temporarily (1), banishing him to the sea in a nutshell, symbolically diminishing death (1).
- Eventually, Jack comes to understand that death is a natural and necessary part of life (1), when Death tells him, 'Without me, there is no life' (1).
- Jack releases Death, and he agrees to spare Jack's mother for a time (1), so the supernatural element is not all evil in this story (1).
- In contrast, *Things My Wife and I Found Hidden in Our House* by Kirsty Logan is a modern supernatural tale (2 – commonality).
- Supernatural element (1) is a deeply sinister and malevolent kelpie, or water spirit (1).
- Narrator, Rain, imagines supernatural items (1) left in their new home are sweet and meant to wish them well (1).
- Rain discovers the pearls on top of the wardrobe and puts them on, she says they are 'as long as a bridle' (1). Simile reminds us of supernatural connection to kelpies and horses; pearls enhance the women's passion and love for each other (1).
- Story becomes progressively more sinister (1) when Alice's hand is burned by a weird copper horse, and Rain is nearly drowned in the bath by the kelpie (1).
- End of the story is particularly sinister and ambiguous (1). The women try to exorcise the kelpie by throwing the gifts/items into the sea (1), and Rain begins to hope that 'women's love was stronger than women's hate' (1). When they come home there is horsehair wrapped around their door handle, suggesting the evil haunting may continue (1).

PART C – SCOTTISH TEXT – POETRY

Text 1 – Poetry

If you choose this text you may not attempt a question on Poetry in Section 2.

Read the poem below and then attempt the following questions.

'Medusa' by Carol Ann Duffy

1   A suspicion, a doubt, a jealousy
     grew in my mind,
     which turned the hairs on my head to filthy snakes,
     as though my thoughts
5   hissed and spat on my scalp.

     My bride's breath soured, stank
     in the grey bags of my lungs.
     I'm foul mouthed now, foul tongued,
     yellow fanged.
10 There are bullet tears in my eyes.
     Are you terrified?

     Be terrified.
     It's you I love,
     perfect man, Greek God, my own;
15 but I know you'll go, betray me, stray
     from home.
     So better by far for me if you were stone.

     I glanced at a buzzing bee,
     a dull grey pebble fell
20 to the ground.
     I glanced at a singing bird,
     a handful of dusty gravel
     spattered down.

     I looked at a ginger cat,
25 a housebrick
     shattered a bowl of milk.
     I looked at a snuffling pig,
     a boulder rolled
     in a heap of shit.

30 I stared in the mirror.
     Love gone bad
     showed me a Gorgon.
     I stared at a dragon.

Fire spewed
35 from the mouth of a mountain.

And here you come
with a shield for a heart
and a sword for a tongue
and your girls, your girls.
40 Wasn't I beautiful?
Wasn't I fragrant and young?

Look at me now.

Questions

1. Look at lines 1 to 5.

   By referring to **two** features of language, explain how the poet suggests Medusa's anger.

   4

2. Look at lines 6 to 11.

   By referring to **two** features of language, show how the poet creates a sense of hostility.

   4

3. Look at lines 18 to 29.

   Identify **one** feature of language and explain how it is used to show Medusa's destructive power.

   2

4. Look at line 42.

   By referring to **one** feature of language, show whether you think this is an effective conclusion to the poem.

   2

5. By referring to this poem and at least **one** other poem by Duffy, show how the poet explores relationships.

   8

OR

Text 2 – Poetry

If you choose this text you may not attempt a question on Poetry in Section 2.

Read the poem below and then attempt the following questions.

'Old Highland Woman' by Norman MacCaig

1   She sits all day by the fire.
How long is it since she opened the door
and stepped outside, confusing
the scuffling hens and the collie
5   dreaming of sheep?
Her walking days are over.

She has come through centuries
of Gaelic labour and loves
and rainy funerals. Her people
10   are assembled in her bones.
She's their summation. *Before her time*
has almost no meaning.

When neighbours call
she laughs a wicked cackle
15   with love in it, as she listens
to the sly bristle of gossip,
relishing the life in it,
relishing the malice, with her hands
lying in her lap like holy psalms
20   that once had a meaning for her, that once
were noble with tunes
she used to sing long ago.

Questions

1. Look at lines 1 to 6.

    Identify **one** feature of language and explain how the poet uses it to show the old woman's decline.

    2

2. Look at lines 7 to 12.

    Referring to **two** features of language, show how the poet creates the sense that the woman represents the history of her people.

    4

3. Look at lines 13 to 18.

    Explain how the poet uses language to create a sense of life and energy. You should refer to **two** features of language.

    4

4. Look at lines 18 to 22.

    Identify **one** feature of language and show how it is used to create a sense of sadness or regret.

    2

5. By referring to this poem and to at least **one** other poem by MacCaig, show how the poet deals with the theme of the past.

    8

OR

Text 3 – Poetry

If you choose this text you may not attempt a question on Poetry in Section 2.

Read the poem below and then attempt the following questions.

From 'Gap Year' by Jackie Kay

I

1 I remember your Moses basket before you were born.
    I'd stare at the fleecy white sheet for days, weeks,
    willing you to arrive, hardly able to believe
    I would ever have a real baby to put in the basket.

5 I'd feel the mound of my tight tub of a stomach,
    and you moving there, foot against my heart,
    elbow in my ribcage, turning, burping, awake, asleep.
    One time I imagined I felt you laugh.

    I'd play you Handel's *Water Music* or Emma Kirkby
10 singing Pergolesi. I'd talk to you, my close stranger,
    call you Tumshie, ask when you were coming to meet me.
    You arrived late, the very hot summer of eighty-eight.

    You had passed the due date string of eights,
    and were pulled out with forceps, blue, floury,
15 on the fourteenth of August on Sunday afternoon.
    I took you home on Monday and lay you in your basket.

II

    Now, I peek in your room and stare at your bed
    hardly able to imagine you back in there sleeping,
    Your handsome face – soft, open. Now you are eighteen,
20 six foot two, away, away in Costa Rica, Peru, Bolivia.

Questions

1. Look at lines 1 to 4.

   By referring to **two** examples of language, show how the poet creates a sense of expectation.

   4

2. Look at lines 5 to 12.

   By referring to **two** examples of language, show how the poet creates a sense of the physical and emotional aspects of the pregnancy.

   4

3. Look at lines 12 to 16.

   By referring to **two** examples of language, show how the poet creates a sense of the late stages of the pregnancy and the birth.

   4

4. Referring to 'Gap Year' and to at least **one** other poem, show how the theme of human relationships is explored in the work of Jackie Kay.

   8

OR

Text 4 – Poetry

If you choose this text you may not attempt a question on Poetry in Section 2.

Read the poem below and then attempt the following questions.

'Love' by Edwin Morgan

1   Love rules. Love laughs. Love marches. Love
        is the wolf that guards the gate.
    Love is the food of music, art, poetry. It
        fills us and fuels us and fires us to create.
5   Love is terror. Love is sweat. Love is bashed
        pillow, crumpled sheet, unenviable fate.
    Love is the honour that kills and saves and nothing
        will ever let that high ambiguity abate.
    Love is the crushed ice that tingles and shivers
10   and clinks fidgin-fain for the sugar-drenched
        absinth to fall on it and alter its state.
            With love you send a probe
            So far from the globe
    No one can name the shoals the voids the belts the
15   zones the drags the flares it signals all to
        leave all and to navigate.

1. Look at lines 1 and 2.

    Referring to **two** features of language, show how the poem begins in a forceful and energetic way.

    4

2. Look at lines 3 to 6.

    Referring to **one** feature of language, explain how the poet shows the power of love.

    2

3. Look at lines 7 to 11.

    Choose **one** image and show how it reveals another, different feature of love.

    2

4. Look at lines 12 to 16.

    Referring to **two** features of language, explain how the poet explores the mystery of love.

    4

5. Referring to this poem and to at least **one** other poem by Morgan, show how the poet deals with the theme of human relationships.

    8

OR

Text 5 – Poetry

If you choose this text you may not attempt a question on Poetry in Section 2.

Read the poem below and then attempt the following questions.

'Little Girls' by Len Pennie

1   The little girl stands on a knife-covered ledge,
    Dancing till blood starts to drip from its edge.
    She's been licking her wounds since the first time she bled,
    Getting judged for each thought she commits in her head.
5   She's been starving herself since she started to eat,
    Connecting the dots of her heart's every beat.
    She's been swimming from fishermen hiding their net,
    And running from wolves that deny they're a threat.

    And the men chime in, 'Silence girl, don't make a fuss,
10   I'd never do this, it's not all of us.'
    To drown out her sorrow, the male chorus sings,
    'It's only a few, you're imagining things.
    You're making this issue seem worse than it is;
    It was only a comment, a gesture, a kiss.
15   It was meant as a compliment – please take a joke,
    Don't bite the hand groping you, savour each poke.
    And the girl learns the axis on which the world spins
    Is powered by people who relish their sins.
    So, she keeps her head down and she learns how to live,
20   To be quiet and not take much more than they give.
    Cause the fragile knife edge she must constantly walk
    Dictates every word she's permitted to talk,
    Each mouthful is measured, each glance not too sly,
    Lest she melt off her wings just from touching the sky.
25   And she'd love to exist as the person she knows
    Lives inside of her mind, but her agony grows.

    As she slowly but surely resigns herself to
    Being smaller and using far less than they do,
    Being meeker and not taking up too much space,
30   Being careful to always remember her place.
    But the little girl vows that the curse will be broken,
    She'll break down the barriers, leave them wide open:
    For the daughters of little girls you wouldn't hear;
    For the children of women you silenced with fear;
35   For our mothers we'll sing till the screams rip the air;
    We are the little girls you couldn't scare.

Questions

1. Look at lines 1 to 8.

   By referring to **two** examples of language, show how the poet creates a sense of danger.

2. Look at lines 9 to 15.

   By referring to **two** examples of language, show how the poet reveals the power of the men.

3. Look at lines 17 to 26.

   By referring to **two** examples of language, explain how the poet shows the restrictions placed on the girl.

4. Referring to 'Little Girls' and to at least **one** other poem from the National 5 Scottish poetry collection, show how the poets explore powerful emotions.

Section 1 Part C Poetry – Model answers
Text 1 – 'Medusa'

1. The first line – 'A suspicion, a doubt, a jealousy' (1) – has a quickening, repetitive, intensifying rhythm that suggests the beginnings of her anger (1).

   The image of her thoughts becoming snakes (1) also indicates her anger (1).

   The poet uses onomatopoeia ('hissed and spat') as well as harsh 's' and 'k' sounds (1) in the last line to convey the anger (1).

2. The metaphor of 'bullet tears' (1) in line 10 suggests danger, aggression and hostility (1).

   The image of the bullets (1) makes me think she has weaponised her sorrow (1).

   Line 11 is a direct and confrontational question – 'Are you terrified?' (1) – and so the tone is particularly hostile (1).

3. The choice of the word 'glanced' suggests a very brief look (1) resulting in the bee being turned to stone, making her seem extremely powerful (1).

4. The line 'Look at me now' is a powerful conclusion. It is a further command or order, similar to 'Be terrified' in line 12 (1).

   The way the line is set on its own and apart from the rest of the poem gives it emphasis and makes us dwell on it: Medusa is horrific to look at now (1).

> The following mini-essay style answer is provided to help you think about the question and the wider text.
>
> The bullet-point version of the answer that follows is intended to help you create your own answer. It is highly recommended that you choose the bullet-point approach for this question type.

5. In 'Medusa', Duffy uses Greek myth to explore how a woman reacts over the long term when she has been let down by a man and their relationship has gone wrong. The poet's language conveys Medusa's anger and her bitterness. So, when she says, 'I know you'll go, betray me, stray/ from home', the internal rhyme in the line emphasises how he will cheat on her. A bitter tone is created by the use of negative words like 'soured', 'dull' and 'shit', and when she uses the image of fire 'spewed/ from the mouth of a mountain' this puts across the immensity of her anger and fury.

   Another dramatic monologue where Duffy uses Greek myth to explore relationships is 'Mrs Midas'. In this poem, Mrs Midas is certainly distressed at how her husband's foolish greed has ruined their relationship. We know this when she says, 'I started to scream'. But she does calm down, and there is even some humour in the poem when she says, 'The toilet I didn't mind', inverting the normal word order to make a joke about the golden toilet.

As 'Mrs Midas' progresses, though, the speaker's tone becomes sad and resigned. She thinks back to the happy 'halcyon days' but sounds more sad than bitter or angry when she calls herself 'the woman who/ married the fool/ who wished for gold'. As the poem comes to an end, she says, 'I miss most, even now, his hands, his warm hands on my skin, his touch'. This poem is sad, tender and wistful, in comparison to Medusa's wild fury and violent hatred.

> Here is the example answer as bullet-points which is the recommended method.

- Duffy uses Greek myth (1) to explore how a woman reacts when she has been let down by a man and their relationship has gone wrong (1).
- 'I know you'll go, betray me, stray/ from home' (1) – internal rhyme emphasises inevitability that he will cheat on her (1).
- Bitter tone created (1) by negative words like 'soured', 'dull' and 'shit' (1).
- Image of fire 'spewed/ from the mouth of a mountain' (1) conveys the immensity of her anger and fury (1).
- Another dramatic monologue where Duffy uses Greek myth to explore relationships is 'Mrs Midas' (2 – commonality).
- Mrs Midas is distressed (1) at how her husband's foolish greed has ruined their relationship (1).
- Word choice emphasises distress (1) – 'I started to scream' (1).
- Narrator calms, and there is some humour (1): 'The toilet I didn't mind', inverting normal word order to create comedic effect (1).
- As 'Mrs Midas' progresses the speaker's tone becomes sad, nostaligic, resigned (1): 'halcyon days' (1).
- Structure sounds progressively more sad than bitter or angry (1) as she calls herself 'the woman who/ married the fool/ who wished for gold' (1).
- Poem closes with sad, wistful, tender tone (1): 'I miss most, even now, his hands, his warm hands on my skin, his touch' (1). Contrast (1) to Medusa's wild fury and violent hatred (1).

Text 2 – 'Old Highland Woman'

1. The opening sentence is very simple and direct (1), using only monosyllabic words to explain the limits of the woman's activity (1).

   Then, a long rhetorical question (1) draws our attention to the fact that it has been a very long time since she was outdoors (1).

   The final sentence – 'Her walking days are over' (1) – is short, blunt and sadly shocking (1).

2. The idea of her travelling through time is metaphorical – 'She has come through centuries' (1) – and suggests that she represents and is similar to her ancestors from the past (1).

   The image of her people being 'assembled in her bones' (1) is slightly sinister but also shows us that she is part of a long history (1).

   The short and direct line, 'She's their summation' (1), makes her seem like a very significant individual (1).

3. The poet describes her laugh as 'a wicked cackle/ with love in it'. This is a paradox, because the words 'wicked' and 'cackle' (1) suggest evil and might make us think of witches, while the phrase 'with love in it' makes us think of pleasure, kindness and her place in her community (1).

   The repetition of 'relishing ... relishing' (1) emphasises her continued enjoyment in gossip and life (1).

4. The repetition of 'that once had a meaning ... that once/ were noble' (1) reminds us that these things are in the past and suggests a sadness at their having disappeared (1).

> The following mini-essay style answer is provided to help you think about the question and the wider text.
>
> The bullet-point version of the answer that follows is intended to help you create your own answer. It is highly recommended that you choose the bullet-point approach for this question type.

5. The woman described in 'Old Highland Woman' represents the past and the poem is mostly sad. It is a lament for this woman who, although still alive, has already lived nearly all of her life. She represents the history of her Gaelic people in the Highlands, and this history is summed up in the lines 'centuries/ of Gaelic labour and loves/ and rainy funerals'. The alliteration in 'labour and loves' links together

the hardships and the good times of the past, while 'rainy funerals' hints at the sadness and misery of human history. The overall tone of the poem is somewhat dark and gloomy.

Another poem by MacCaig that deals with the past is 'Aunt Julia'. This is generally a happier poem, dealing with family history and creating a vivid, energetic portrait of the poet's Gaelic-speaking aunt:

> Aunt Julia spoke Gaelic
> Very loud and very fast
>> I could not answer her –
>> I could not understand her

The language is simple and direct and shows us that the poet as a boy was a little bewildered by his aunt's language and energy. As in 'Old Highland Woman', this suggests that the past is mysterious and enigmatic.

Aunt Julia is characterised in the poem through a series of associations. The metaphorical line 'She was men's boots' makes me think she was practical and possibly slightly eccentric.

Towards the end of the poem, the poet returns to the ideas of language and communication:

> Aunt Julia spoke Gaelic
> very loud and very fast.
> By the time I had learned
>> a little, she lay
>> silenced in the absolute black
>> of a sandy grave
>> at Luskentyre.

The forceful, energetic rhythm of 'very loud and very fast' is in contrast to the sad finality of 'silenced in the absolute black/ of a sandy grave'. This poem ends similarly to 'Old Highland Woman', with a sadness and a wistful regret as the poet feels he can never reach or fully understand the past of his own family and his own people.

Here is the example answer as bullet-points which is the recommended method.

- Woman in 'Old Highland Woman' represents the past (1) and the poem is mostly sad (1).
- Lament for a woman (1) who, although still alive, has already lived nearly all of her life (1).

- History summed up in the lines 'centuries/ of Gaelic labour and loves/ and rainy funerals'. The alliteration in 'labour and loves' (1) links together the hardships and the good times of the past (1).
- 'Rainy funerals' (1) hints at the sadness and misery of human history (1).
- Overall tone of this poem (1) is somewhat dark and gloomy (1).
- Another poem by MacCaig that deals with the past is 'Aunt Julia' (2 – commonality).
- This is generally a happier poem (1), dealing with family history and creating a vivid, energetic portrait (1) of the poet's Gaelic-speaking aunt: 'Aunt Julia spoke Gaelic/ Very loud and very fast'.
- Simple and direct language (1) shows us that poet was bewildered by his aunt's language and energy (1).
- As in 'Old Highland Woman', this (1) suggests that the past is mysterious and enigmatic (1).
- Aunt Julia is characterised in the poem through a series of associations (1); metaphorical 'She was men's boots' suggests she was practical and eccentric (1).
- Towards the end of the poem (1), poet returns to the ideas of language and communication (1).
- Forceful, energetic rhythm of 'very loud and very fast' (1) is in contrast to the sad finality of 'silenced in the absolute black/ of a sandy grave' (1).
- Poem ends similarly to 'Old Highland Woman' (1) with sadness and wistful regret (1) as the poet feels he can't reach or understand the past of his own family (1) or his own people (1).

Text 3 – 'Gap Year'

1. 'I'd stare at the fleecy white sheet for days, weeks' (1) – insistent rhythm creates sense of expectation (1).

   Intensifying effect (1) from choice of words 'days' and 'weeks' creates sense of expectation (1).

2. 'mound' of the stomach – metaphor (1) makes stomach seem very large, possibly uncomfortable (1).

   'tight tub' of stomach – metaphor again (1) suggests pressure and discomfort, making the skin seem taut (1). Alliteration emphasises the phrase (1).

   Strange juxtapositions (placing together) of images 'foot against my heart' and 'elbow in my ribcage' (1) suggests odd, incongruous positions of the bodies of mother and son (1).

   The poet uses present participles ('turning, burping') (1) to create a sense of activity and movement (1).

   Contrast ('awake, asleep') (1) is used to show different moods of the pregnancy (1).

   The poet uses an oxymoron ('close stranger') (1) to show the peculiarity of the relationship between the mother and her unborn child (1).

   The child is 'close', because it is in her womb (1), and also maybe because she already feels close to her unborn baby. It is at the same time a stranger, because she has not met it yet (1).

   She uses an affectionate Scots word/metaphor (1) as a name for her unborn baby – 'Tumshie', meaning 'turnip' (1).

3. Internal rhymes and repetition are used in the lines 'You arrived late, the very hot summer of eighty-eight./ You had passed the due date string of eights,' (1). These rhymes stand out within the extract, because there are no other rhymes. They quicken the rhythm and create a sense of tension or urgency as the birth approaches (1).

   The phrase 'due date string of eights' is memorable and unusual, telling us that the baby must have been due on August 8th, 1988 (1). The metaphor of the 'string' makes me think of the looping figures of the 'eights' (1).

   Adjectives used to describe the new-born baby are unusual: 'blue, floury' (1). 'Blue' suggests the baby may have been short of oxygen at the point of birth, while 'floury' makes us think of something pleasant, perhaps sweet, comforting (1).

'I took you home on Monday and lay you in your basket.' This sentence is very simple, and mostly monosyllabic (1). It refers back to the idea of the Moses basket from the beginning of the extract and suggests calm and simplicity following the birth (1).

> The following mini-essay style answer is provided to help you think about the question and the wider text.
>
> The bullet-point version of the answer that follows is intended to help you create your own answer. It is highly recommended that you choose the bullet-point approach for this question type.

4. The first part of 'Gap Year' focuses on the sense of excitement and anticipation felt by the mother before the birth of her son. The extract is full of tenderness, though, and has an affectionate, light tone. This is created by the use of the pet name 'Tumshie', the way the poem is addressed to her son and uses the pronoun 'you' throughout, and the tender detail of laying the baby in his basket.

As 'Gap Year' goes on, it describes what her son does as he grows up and goes into detail about the writer's pride and anxiety when he travels across the world to South America. The poet includes an echo of the early part of the poem, hinting at her anxiety: 'And now you are not coming home till four weeks after/ your due date.' But there is also a clear feeling of pride in the poem:

> My heart soars like the birds in your bright blue skies.
> My love glows like the sunrise over the lost city.
> I have a son out in the big wide world.

The poet uses repetitive patterning to emphasise the pride and joy she feels, now that her son has grown up and is travelling and experiencing the world.

Another poem by Jackie Kay dealing with human relationships is 'Keeping Orchids'. This is also a poem about family relationships, but this time exploring the poet's confused and uncomfortable feelings after she has met her birth mother for the first time. 'Keeping Orchids' opens with a seemingly confusing statement and shows that the two women have just met as adults: 'The orchids my mother gave me when we first met/ are still alive, twelve days later.'

The poem uses the image of the orchids to suggest certain things about motherhood, and her relationship with her birth mother. The buds 'remain closed as secrets', hinting that there are many things about her past and her mother that she does not know. She carries them like a 'baby in a shawl', reminding us of the fact that her mother must once have carried her, but gave her up for adoption. When she knocks the vase containing the orchids over, there is a reference to 'All the broken waters'. This is a slightly bitter-sounding reference to a mother's waters breaking before birth.

'Keeping Orchids' ends with the lines 'Boiling water makes the flowers live longer. So does/ Cutting the stems with a sharp knife.' This image suggests discomfort, pain or violence. We are left with the sense that her feelings for her birth mother cause her pain, and it may be that she wants to cut off her contact with her.

Altogether, 'Keeping Orchids' is a dark and sometimes unhappy-sounding poem, and is in stark contrast to the joyful, happy relationship described in 'Gap Year'.

Here is the example answer as bullet-points which is the recommended method.

- 'Gap Year' focuses (1) on the excitement and anticipation felt by the mother before the birth of her son (1).

- Extract is full of tenderness and has an affectionate, light tone (1) – use of pet name 'Tumshie' (1), poem uses the pronoun 'you' throughout (1), and tender detail of laying the baby in his basket (1).

- As 'Gap Year' goes on (1), it describes what her son does as he grows up and the writer's pride and anxiety when he travels across the world to South America (1). Poet includes an echo of the early part of poem, hinting at her anxiety: 'And now you are not coming home till four weeks after/ your due date.' (1) But there is also a clear feeling of pride (1):

  My heart soars like the birds in your bright blue skies.
  My love glows like the sunrise over the lost city.
  I have a son out in the big wide world.

- The poet uses repetitive patterning (1) to emphasise the pride and joy (1) she feels.

- Another poem by Jackie Kay dealing with human relationships is 'Keeping Orchids' (2 – commonality).

- 'Keeping Orchids' deals with the poet's confused and uncomfortable feelings (1) on meeting her birth mother for the first time (1).

- Poem opens with a seemingly confusing statement (1) and shows that the two women have just met as adults: 'The orchids my mother gave me when we first met/ are still alive, twelve days later.' (1)

- Poem uses the image (1) of the orchids to suggest certain things about motherhood, and her relationship with her birth mother (1).

- Buds 'remain closed as secrets' (1), hinting that there are many things about her past and her mother that she does not know (1).

- The simile she carries them like a 'baby in a shawl' (1), reminds us of the fact that her mother must once have carried her (1), but gave her up for adoption.

- When she knocks the vase containing the orchids over, there is a reference to 'All the broken waters' (1) – this is a bitter-sounding reference to a mother's waters breaking before birth (1).
- 'Keeping Orchids' ends with the lines 'Boiling water makes the flowers live longer. So does/ Cutting the stems with a sharp knife.' (1) Image suggests discomfort, pain or violence (1).
- Sense that her feelings for her birth mother cause her pain (1), and it may be that she wants to cut off her contact with her (1).
- 'Keeping Orchids' is a dark and sometimes unhappy-sounding poem in contrast (1) to the joyful, happy relationship described in 'Gap Year' (1).

Text 4 – 'Love'

1. The poem begins with three very short sentences/statements, each starting with the word 'love' followed by a verb (1). The effect is punchy, like staccato notes in music (1). The first line runs on into line two (1), creating a pause for suspense (1), and then love is compared in a metaphor (1) to a 'wolf' – this image is surprising and hints at danger (1).

2. The powerful, falling rhythm of 'It/ fills us and fuels us and fires us to create' (1) conveys a real sense of the power of love (1). The force of this line is also enhanced (1) by the alliteration and repetition (1).

3. The metaphor of love as the ice in a glass awaiting the absinth (1) suggests a transformation or an almost chemical change that happens when two separate elements or people are united in love (1).

   The poet makes it seem as if the ice is waiting in nervous anticipation (1) through the listing of verbs 'tingles and shivers/ and clinks' (1).

4. In lines 12 to 16, the poet creates yet another metaphor for love, this time comparing it to a space probe being launched into the cosmos (1). This image enhances the sense of mystery and excitement as the probe voyages through unexplored regions of space such as 'voids', 'belts' and 'zones' (1).

   The wording or the grammar at the close of the poem may be deliberately confusing (1), mirroring the confusion felt by the person in love – 'it signals all to/ leave all and to navigate' – but also showing us how important and valuable it is for us to 'navigate' love and to find our way through it (1).

> The following mini-essay style answer is provided to help you think about the question and the wider text.
>
> The bullet-point version of the answer that follows is intended to help you create your own answer. It is highly recommended that you choose the bullet-point approach for this question type.

5. 'Love' explores some of the energising, exciting and passionate aspects of human love and human relationships. The poem shows that love can be overwhelming and joyful, and uses powerful rhythms, rhymes and alliteration to create a noisy and energetic sense of what love can be. Images like 'Love is bashed/ pillow, crumpled sheet' suggest physical passion, and word choices like the Scots 'fidgin-fain' or 'sugar-drenched' add a touch of humour and sweetness. 'Love' is an abstract poem about what love can be like for all kinds of different people.

   By comparison, 'Strawberries' is a more personal poem written about the experience of a specific individual and addressed to their lover: 'There were never strawberries/ like the ones we had/ that sultry afternoon ...'. The way the voice in this poem seems to speak directly to their lover is more intimate than in 'Love'. 'Strawberries' moves on in short lines, telling the story of the afternoon in a step-by-step way, as if not wishing to spoil the pleasure by rushing. The strawberries' sweetness represents the sweetness of love, and the eating of the strawberries represents the physical love between the two people: 'not hurrying the feast/ for the one to come'. Towards the end of the poem, a lightning storm symbolises the natural passion between the lovers, and the poem ends with a command – 'let the storm wash the plates' – suggesting both abandon and relaxed contentment.

'Love' is about love in general, and how human beings experience love, while 'Strawberries' is about a specific day and a specific love between two individuals. Both poems are, however, celebrations of the power and the joy of love.

Here is the example answer as bullet-points which is the recommended method.

- 'Love' explores energising, exciting and passionate aspects (1) of human love and human relationships (1).
- Powerful rhythms, rhymes and alliteration (1) to create a noisy and energetic sense of how joyful and exciting love can be (1).
- Image/metaphor 'Love is bashed/ pillow, crumpled sheet' (1) suggests physical passion (1).
- Word choices 'fidgin-fain' or 'sugar-drenched' (1) add humour and sense of sweetness (1).
- 'Love' is an abstract poem (1) about what love can be like for all kinds of different people (1).
- By comparison, 'Strawberries' is a personal poem written about the experience of a specific individual and addressed to their lover (2 – commonality).
- 'There were never strawberries/ like the ones we had/ that sultry afternoon ...' – poetic voice (1) in this poem seems to speak directly to their lover, is more intimate than in 'Love' (1).
- 'Strawberries' moves on in short lines (1), revealing events in step-by-step way, as if not wishing to spoil the pleasure by rushing (1).
- The strawberries' sweetness represents the sweetness of love (1), and the eating of the strawberries represents the physical love between the two people (1): 'not hurrying the feast/ for the one to come'.
- Lightning storm symbolises (1) the natural passion between the lovers (1).
- Poem ends with command – 'let the storm wash the plates' (1) – suggesting abandon and contentment (1).

Text 5 – 'Little Girls'

1. The metaphor of the girl standing on a 'knife-covered ledge' (1) creates a sense of danger (1). The image suggests the girl is in a very precarious situation (1), and the reference to knives suggests pain or violence (1).

    The imagery at the close of the first verse (1) suggests further threat and danger (1). The 'fishermen hiding their net' (1) seem to want to trap the girl (1), while the 'wolves that deny they're a threat' (1) seem predatory and sinister (1).

2. The first words the men utter form a command/order – 'Silence girl …' – (1) suggesting they are in a position of absolute power (1). The men are described as a 'chorus' (1), so they speak together with an overpowering, collective voice (1).

    The poet introduces speech to show how the men gaslight the girl (1): '… you're imagining things./ You're making this issue seem worse than it is …' (1). Only the men are given a voice at this point in the poem (1); the girl does not reply (1). The girl is alone (1), while the men are a group (1).

3. The powerful, regular rhythm and the rhyming couplets (1) create an intense effect and a sense of speed and fear as the girl begins to understand the restrictions she is living with (1):

    > And the girl learns the axis on which the world spins
    > Is powered by people who relish their sins.

    The girl would like to live out her dreams, but the reference to the myth of Icarus, who burned his wings by flying too close to the sun (1), shows that she feels unable or is still too afraid to take this risk (1).

The following mini-essay style answer is provided to help you think about the question and the wider text.

The bullet-point version of the answer that follows is intended to help you create your own answer. It is highly recommended that you choose the bullet-point approach for this question type.

---

4. 'Little Girls' explores the powerful, overwhelming negative emotions felt by young women who have been badly treated by men. The first two verses describe the horror and the devastating effects of misogynistic behaviour. Verse three continues in this way by using repetition to show how the girl tries continually to avoid drawing attention to herself – 'Being smaller … Being meeker … Being careful …'. But the speaker of the poem eventually gathers her strength in the final six lines. The poet shows the speaker's strength and passion by using anaphora in 'For the

daughters ... For the children of women ... For our mothers ...' to include all the women who have been wrongly treated. The poem ends with a rallying cry:

> For our mothers we'll sing till the screams rip the air;
> We are the little girls you couldn't scare.

The choice of words such as 'screams' and 'rip' show the speaker's strength, her resolve and her furious passion. The final line, which seems like it is shouted or even screamed, shows the girls have finally overcome their fear and have asserted themselves and their rights.

A very different poem/song that also deals with strong emotion is Robert Burns' 'A Red, Red Rose'. The singer/speaker communicates their love for the subject of the poem through the very simple and natural similes of the 'red, red rose' and the melody 'sweetly play'd in tune'. These images suggest pleasure and happiness, and focus on sweetness, harmony and beauty.

In the second verse, the speaker/singer expresses the depth of their emotion through simple repetitions ('As fair art thou ...' and 'So deep in love am I ...') but the verse ends with an awe-inspiring image of their love enduring until the end of the world: 'Till aa' the seas gang dry'. This surreal and almost impossible image communicates the vastness and endlessness of the love felt by the speaker.

The song/poem intensifies further in verse three, with the repetition of 'Till a' the seas gang dry ...', followed by further surreal images of the end of time such as 'the rocks melt wi' the sun' and 'the sands o' life shall run', again declaring their love will continue until the world's end.

These poems deal with the most powerful of emotions: anger and love. Len Pennie uses language to create a passionate, furious poem that ends in a powerful rallying cry to women to stand up for their rights, while Robert Burns' song communicates tenderness, devotion and a love so strong that it will last forever.

Here is the example answer as bullet-points which is the recommended method.

- First two verses of 'Little Girls' (1) describe the horror and devastating effects of misogynistic behaviour (1).
- Verse three continues, using repetition (1) to show how the girl avoids drawing attention to herself – 'Being smaller ... Being meeker ... Being careful ...' (1).
- Speaker eventually gathers strength in final six lines. Poet shows speaker's strength and passion by using anaphora in 'For the daughters ... For the children of women ... For our mothers ...' (1) to include all women who have been wrongly treated (1).

- Poem ends with a rallying cry (1):

  > For our mothers we'll sing till the screams rip the air;
  > We are the little girls you couldn't scare (1).

  Choice of words – 'screams' and 'rip' (1) – shows speaker's strength, resolve and furious passion (1).
- Final line seems like it is shouted or screamed (1), shows the girls have finally overcome their fear and have asserted themselves and their rights (1).
- A very different poem/song that also deals with strong emotion is Robert Burns' 'A Red, Red Rose' (2 – commonality).
- Singer/speaker communicates their love for the subject of the poem through simple, natural similes 'red, red rose' and the melody 'sweetly play'd in tune' (1). Images suggest pleasure and happiness, and focus on sweetness, harmony and beauty (1).
- In second verse, speaker/singer expresses the depth of their emotion (1) through simple repetitions ('As fair art thou ...' and 'So deep in love am I ...') (1).
- Verse ends with an awe-inspiring image of their love enduring until the end of the world (1): 'Till aa' the seas gang dry'. This surreal and almost impossible image communicates the vastness and endlessness of the love felt by the speaker (1).
- Song/poem intensifies further in verse three – repetition of 'Till a' the seas gang dry ...' (1) followed by further surreal images of the end of time such as 'the rocks melt wi' the sun' and 'the sands o' life shall run' (1), again declaring their love will continue until the world's end (1).

1 | Drama – *Black Watch* by Gregory Burke

Q Choose a play which explores an important idea or theme.
Say briefly what the main idea or theme is and explain how the writer explores this idea or theme.

Gregory Burke's powerful and moving play *Black Watch* deals with the final stages of the history of the famous Scottish infantry regiment during the Iraq War in 2004. The idea of injustice is a key concern in this play. As the drama develops, the soldier characters suffer a variety of injustices, and we as an audience feel a deep sense of sympathy for them.

One important theme in the play is the idea that the soldiers are suffering injustice at the hands of politicians. These soldiers have been sent on an extremely dangerous mission. An early scene uses actual quotations from real politicians who were involved at the time. Geoff Hoon, the defence secretary, claims that the leader of the Scottish Nationalists seeks to take 'political advantage' of the situation, while Alex Salmond claims '800 Scottish soldiers are replacing 4,000 American marines'. As an audience sympathetic to the plight of the characters, we are unsettled by this warning about the danger of the situation, which ironically proves to be true when three of the soldiers are killed in an ambush at the end of the play. Emails home from a commanding officer to his wife show the private worries and stresses of those in charge of the 'regimental family' in a realistic way. This again makes us feel deeply sympathetic to the soldiers, and angry with the politicians who have sent them to Iraq: 'My darling … every lunatic terrorist for miles around will descend on us like bees to honey'. The officer's tender tone when talking to his wife in this message is particularly touching. The metaphor comparing the terrorists to bees is appropriate, because the terrorists are dangerous and capable of doing harm, just like bees with their sting.

The play is also concerned with the history of the regiment. The scene entitled 'Fashion' takes the audience through 300 years of regimental history in the space of a few minutes. The cast dress Cammy in a series of different uniforms, representing different periods from the Battle of Culloden through to WWI and WWII. Cammy talks about a metaphorical 'Golden Thread', which symbolises historical continuity in the regiment. Cammy's father served in the regiment, as did his grandfather and his great-grandfather. The play's emphasis on history and the way the characters value history and tradition is deeply ironic because, as an audience, we know that the government have already decided to amalgamate the regiment, breaking the vital 'Golden Thread'. This is another injustice which makes us feel sympathy towards the characters.

Cammy's character is an interesting one. Although he is certainly a tough soldier, he also comes across at times as being boyish, even vulnerable (he is afraid his mother will see him smoking when he appears on a TV news programme). He is sensitive and thoughtful about the deployment in Iraq, saying 'this is just plain old fashioned bullying, like', and goes on to make a passionate, heartfelt criticism of the war:

'It's a buzz, you're in a war, ay but you're no really doing the job you're trained for it's no like they're a massive threat tay you or tay your country. We're invading their country ...'.

Cammy's comments show us that the deployment is unjust for the Black Watch soldiers, and also perhaps that it is unjust for the Iraqis they are fighting against. He is sickened, for instance, by the overwhelming firepower used by the Americans in the scene 'Allies', which is based on the aerial bombardment of the town of Falluja.

The greatest injustice of all, however, comes at the end of the play, when three soldiers, Fraz, Kenzie and Sergeant Munroe, are killed in a suicide bombing. Humour is used just before the bombing, as the soldiers joke about their sergeant while he investigates a car at a road block, saying he is 'channelling his inner traffic warden'. This makes the explosion all the more unexpected, shocking and frightening. In the theatre, the blast has incredible volume. The men's bodies then float horrifically, like blood-covered ghosts suspended in the theatre, haunting the audience. A Gaelic lament is sung, which again makes us think sadly of the loss of the men, and the fact that the history of their regiment has come to an end. We are left wondering whether their deaths have served any purpose at all.

Gregory Burke has succeeded in creating a play which shows clearly the injustices suffered by these soldiers, who are put on an extremely dangerous mission while their regiment is being amalgamated. They question the war they are fighting, and in the end they suffer the ultimate injustice when three of them are killed for no real reason. The playwright has used irony, dialogue, humour and extracts from real media broadcasts in order to develop this theme of injustice, and to enhance our feeling of sympathy for the characters.

Q Choose a novel or a short story where there is an admirable character.
By referring to appropriate techniques, explain how the writer makes this character admirable.

Harper Lee's classic 1960 novel *To Kill a Mockingbird* has become famous around the world for its depiction of racism in the United States during the nineteen-thirties. *To Kill a Mockingbird* features an admirable character called Atticus Finch. Atticus is a lawyer in the small town of Maycomb in Alabama.

He is the father of Scout Finch, the young narrator of the story.

Atticus is a widower, his young wife having died when their children were very small. He works hard as a lawyer in the town and he is a dependable and calm – if slightly boring – father to Scout and her brother Jem. Scout says of him: 'we found our father satisfactory: he played with us, read to us, and treated us with courteous detachment'. Atticus seems an unlikely hero, and a less than inspirational father to Scout and Jem. Scout's choice of the word 'satisfactory' seems to suggest that she thinks he could be better. It is as if she damns her father with faint praise.

At almost 50, Atticus is older than the other fathers in the community, and therefore less strong or physically able. We get the impression that Scout is slightly embarrassed by him, when she says things like 'Atticus was feeble …' or 'Our father didn't do anything … that could possibly arouse the admiration of anyone'. This statement later proves to be ironic, for Atticus shows that he has tremendous moral courage that more than compensates for his lack of physical strength.

The children begin to realise that there may be more to their father than meets the eye one day when a dangerous, rabid dog appears in the street. The local policeman is called to shoot the dog, but he hands the rifle to Atticus, who takes the difficult shot and kills the dog instantly. This is an important point in the author's characterisation of Atticus, and we see real development of the character. Scout and Jem are amazed and begin to realise their father may have hidden talents and capabilities. Miss Maudie points out to the children that their father is 'civilised in his heart'. Her comment links to the key theme of civilisation, and what it really means. The white Maycomb community like to think of themselves as 'civilised', but most of them are unashamedly racist in their outlook. (It is no coincidence that a black worker, Zeebo, is later summoned to dispose of the dangerous corpse of the infected dog.)

Atticus takes a courageous moral stand when he agrees to defend a black man, Tom Robinson, who has been accused of raping a white girl. The scene where Atticus' courage comes most obviously to the fore is where he chooses to spend the evening sitting reading outside the Maycomb jail, which we are told has a 'good, solid respectable look' and 'no stranger would ever suspect it was full of n*****s'. These comments show the hypocrisy and racism of the community. The jail is a symbol of respectability on the outside and evil racism on the inside — like most of the people in Maycomb.

Despite being older and physically weak, Atticus shows great moral and physical courage in defending Tom, who is inside, from a lynch mob who appear outside the jail. The mob is described as having a 'smell of stale whisky and pig-pen'. These men are intent on murdering Tom and are truly the worst kind of 'redneck' racists. But Atticus is polite and reasons with them, refusing to let them in to harm Tom. Scout's brave (and naïve) intervention charms the men and diverts them from their evil purpose. We only understand the terrible tension of the moment afterwards, as the calm and brave Atticus leans against the jail with his face to the wall, exhausted, frightened and only temporarily relieved. He and his daughter have saved an innocent man from certain death at the hands of a racist mob.

Atticus' moral and ethical strengths come to the fore in the closing stages of the story where he mounts a powerful and compelling defence of Tom Robinson. He is labelled a 'n****r lover' by the racists, simply for taking the case on. At the end of the day, he cannot save the innocent Tom, who is eventually killed during a desperate escape bid. But Atticus has left a small mark of change and progress in his racist community. This is best summed up in his metaphorical comment to Scout that the community has made a 'baby step' forwards by listening to and considering Tom's case.

Atticus has stood against almost the entire community and establishment, facing great personal danger and danger to his own children, in order to stand up for an innocent man. Harper Lee has used dialogue, irony and careful exposition of character in her novel to help us to understand the difficulties that Atticus overcomes: he is truly an admirable character.

Q Choose a poem that features a chance meeting or an unexpected event.
By referring to appropriate techniques, show how this chance meeting or unexpected event is explored.

Edwin Morgan's 'Trio' is a poem which begins with a description of a chance meeting and goes on to reflect on deeper ideas suggested by this meeting.

The poem opens with a description of the chance meeting, which is between the poet/speaker and a group of three young people who are 'Coming up Buchanan Street, quickly, on a sharp winter evening', in the run up to Christmas. The rhythm of this opening line is energetic and lively, starting the poem off in a positive way as the people walk quickly through the cold. The poem continues in this positive mood, as we are told: 'the three of them are laughing, their breath rises/ in a cloud of happiness'. The poet's use of enjambment delays and emphasises the description of happiness, and the metaphor comparing the cloud of their breath to some kind of visible 'happiness' also adds to the bright, festive mood. The young man is carrying a guitar which, it seems, will be a present for someone. One of the girls has a very young baby, and the other girl is carrying a chihuahua – a tiny dog.

The poet includes a snippet of dialogue, as the man says, 'Wait till he sees this but!'. The use of the word 'but' as an interjection is a feature of Glasgow dialect, and the exclamation adds to the sense of excitement, happiness and anticipation at the beginning of the poem. The poet then goes on to describe the chihuahua, the baby and the guitar in turn. The chihuahua has a 'tiny Royal Stewart tartan coat like a teapot-holder'. As well as suggesting something particularly special or regal, this line – with the simile of the 'teapot-holder' – gives us the impression that the dog is warm, cosy and happy on this very cold night. Another simile is used to describe the baby: 'all bright eyes and mouth like favours in a fresh sweet cake'. This suggests the baby's face is smooth and even, like the icing on a cake, and that its eyes and mouth stand out like cake decorations in their sweet beauty. The guitar is 'tied at the neck ... with a brisk sprig of mistletoe'. Assonance has been used here to emphasise the words 'brisk' and 'sprig', again in a bright, cheery-sounding way. Then, a three-part structure and further exclamations are used in what is the most positive sounding line of the poem so far: 'Orphean sprig! Melting baby! Warm chihuahua!'. This line has a celebratory, rhetorical sound, and is a real climax to the first part of the poem.

From this point on, the poem starts to become much more reflective. It moves on from the straightforward positive description of the people to a more thoughtful section about Christmas, and life itself. There have been some hints so far that link the meeting with these people and the nativity story. There are three of them, and they are bearing gifts, like the three wise men. There is also a baby, as in the nativity story. The poet suggests that these three have an almost magical power, saying 'the vale of tears is powerless before you', meaning that evil, misfortune or unhappiness have no power over the happiness of the three. Yet they are not especially religious or Christian, for the poet says: 'Whether Christ is born, or not born, you/ put paid to fate'. The three, although happy, are not really thinking about the religious aspect of Christmas. This reflective section of the poem introduces agnostic or humanist ideas and celebrates the power that human happiness can have over the unhappy things that can sometimes happen to us: what the poet describes in a disturbing metaphor as the 'Monsters of the year'.

So, this poem begins with a positive and seemingly simple description of a chance meeting and goes on to reflect on deeper ideas about Christmas and Christianity. The poem seems to conclude that human happiness and positivity – represented by birth, love of animals and music – are powerful enough in themselves to overcome pain or adversity – the 'Monsters of the year' – that we may face in our everyday lives.

Part 3 Performance – Spoken Language

Performance – Spoken Language: What is it?

As the name suggests, 'Spoken Language' is the part of your National 5 course where you are required to demonstrate your speaking skills.

Spoken language is assessed in your school or centre by your teacher.

There is no mark assigned to this part of the course; you will simply be awarded a pass once you have met the success criteria.

The success criteria for this part of the course are as follows:

1. You are required to talk, delivering detailed content and language.
2. You should be able to use some non-verbal aspects of communication such as gestures, eye-contact or variety in your tone of voice for emphasis.
3. You should also be able to demonstrate your skills in listening, by responding in some detail to questions or contributions from other people who have been listening to your talk.

There are two options for your assessment in spoken language. You may take part in a group discussion where you will be assessed on your contributions to the discussion and your responses to the contributions or questions of others. Alternatively, you may deliver an individual presentation or part of a group presentation to an audience and answer questions or respond to contributions from the audience on the material you have presented.

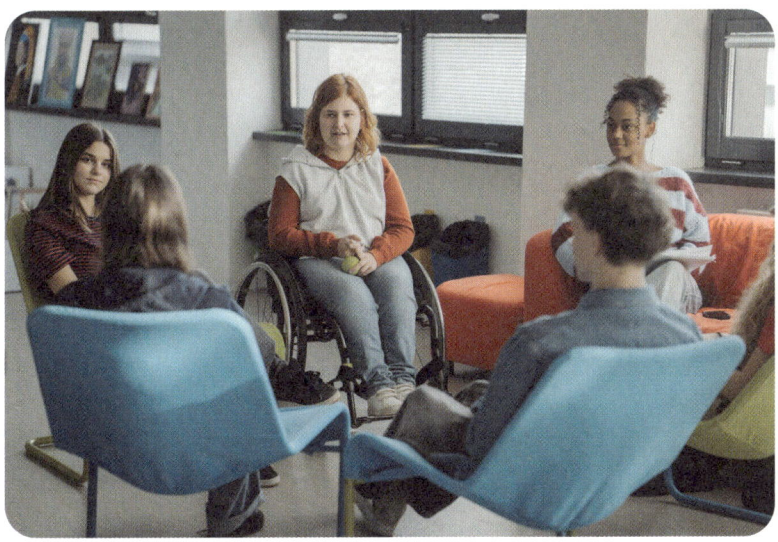

Spoken language key data

Options	Contribute to group discussion Deliver individual presentation Deliver part of a group presentation
Length of talk	No set length, but 5 minutes is more than adequate
Assessment	In class by your teacher
Number of marks available	Not marked but assessed as pass or fail
Percentage of the total marks available for National 5 English	Does not contribute to your overall grade/mark but you do have to pass to complete your National 5 and gain your course award

Performance – Spoken Language: How to do it

Developing your spoken language, and, importantly, developing your confidence in speaking in front of a small audience are very useful skills for life after school. The ability to talk to others in a formal or semi-formal situation is a particularly useful skill for many workplaces and countless other situations in adult life.

It is very common and very natural to feel some anxiety about the performance aspect of this part of your National 5 course. Nearly everyone experiences some nerves or anxiety about talking in front of other people – even teachers and other professionals who have to talk to large audiences regularly.

Once they have gone through the pressure of preparing and delivering a short talk or presentation, most people feel a sense of accomplishment. Their confidence grows in the long term. There is a lot to be said for pushing yourself 'out of your comfort zone'.

Candidate question

Can I do an individual presentation for spoken language on the same topic I researched for my discursive writing piece?

A Yes, you can. If you have struck on a topic that really interests or inspires you, this might be the ideal topic to talk about in a presentation, especially if you have developed a little expert knowledge. Your portfolio piece will also have a structure you can follow for your talk.

With each opportunity you take to speak in a group or publicly, the more your confidence will grow, and the less anxiety you will feel. You may never be completely free from anxiety when speaking, but a little anxiety is useful and can really help to keep you alert and improve your performance.

I'm autistic and I am very passionately interested in some specific topics. Can I talk about one of these topics?

A Absolutely! You should make the most of your strengths and enthusiasms. If you can deliver a presentation on something you love and have specialist knowledge of, you will do well.

There are ways you can prepare for your assessment that will help you to minimise any nervousness you may be experiencing, and make sure you achieve the pass you are looking for.

You should consider the following ideas as you prepare.

If you are preparing for an individual presentation:

1. Choose a topic that you are especially interested in, a topic that is close to your heart.
2. Research your topic in the same way as you would research for a piece of discursive writing.
3. Create a simple electronic presentation or use cards to help you to structure your talk.
4. When the time comes to perform, try to enjoy being in the spotlight! The process can be exciting and energising if you are able to communicate some new thoughts, ideas or perspectives to your audience.
5. You may have developed some expert knowledge of the topic, so consider any audience questions as a further opportunity for you to interact and communicate.

If you are preparing for a group discussion:

1. Spend some time beforehand thinking about the topic of the discussion and prepare some things that you would like to say. A group discussion may well be based on work you are doing in class for the Critical Reading paper, so you will be able to prepare your thoughts and contributions.
2. Be sure to contribute during the discussion. Find an opportunity during the discussion and make your points. You will have to take the initiative!
3. Listen carefully while the discussion is going on. Remember, you are also required to show that you have been listening and considering the views and contributions of others in your group.

Portfolio Writing: What is it?

Portfolio writing is the part of the course where you produce and submit one piece of your own extended writing.

You will plan, draft and write your piece over a period of time, and it will be submitted for what is known as 'external' assessment by markers.

Portfolio writing is not part of the examination, but it does count towards your final mark and grade for National 5 English. Most people really enjoy the creative process of planning and crafting a piece of writing, and for many people their National 5 portfolio piece turns out to be the best piece of writing of their school career to date.

Your portfolio writing will be assessed and marked out of 15. The mark is then scaled up to a mark out of 30. This means that the portfolio writing is worth a potential 30 marks, or 30% of the total available marks for National 5.

Your teacher will monitor the process of the production of your portfolio piece, discussing your choice of topic and looking over your early notes and plans. The first draft of your piece will be completed in school under supervision. Your teacher will give you some feedback on your first draft, but they cannot give you specific corrections or suggestions – the work must be your own and you must demonstrate your own ability to write and communicate clearly with accurate spelling and structure. So, plan carefully and use a dictionary to check the spellings of any words – particularly any new or specialised words – that you intend to use. Your final draft will be completed under some supervision.

Your finished piece of portfolio writing should be no longer than 1000 words. It must be entirely your own work. If you choose to write one of the 'discursive' options, you must acknowledge any sources you use in a bibliography. You mustn't use AI, and you mustn't incorporate text that has been written by anyone else or published elsewhere – unless you are quoting from another text or source and using clear quotation marks.

 KEY CONCEPTS

A **bibliography** is simply a list of sources (books, articles, websites, interviews, etc.) that you may have consulted when preparing to write your portfolio piece. If you list or declare your sources this helps your reader to understand how your thinking has been shaped. It also helps to prove that your work is your own and hasn't been plagiarised (copied from someone or somewhere else). If you choose to use another person's words or a quote from a website or book this is OK, but you must use inverted commas to identify the quote.

Candidate question

Do I have to include my title and bibliography in my word count?

A No, your title and bibliography are not included in the word count. Only the main body of your portfolio writing should be counted.

Whichever genre of writing you opt for, portfolio writing gives you the opportunity to express yourself and to learn about writing while transferring some of the skills you have been learning through the RUAE and Critical Reading parts of the course.

Your piece of writing should either be broadly 'creative' or broadly 'discursive'. The following tables list the different possibilities available to you.

Creative writing options	Description
personal	Where you write from your own point of view about a real event, circumstance, situation or experience (often overlaps with reflective)
reflective	Where you write detailing your own thoughts about an experience, an idea or a concept (often overlaps with personal)
prose fiction	Writing a short story of your own, or even a section of your own novel
poetry	You may choose to write and submit a single poem
dramatic script	You may choose to write an extract or scene from a play

Discursive writing options	Description
persuasive	Where you set out to persuade your reader of your point of view on a topic, issue or phenomenon
argumentative	Where you explore two or more points of view on a topic, issue or phenomenon
report	Where you write to describe an event, a process or a plan in close detail
transactional or informative	Where you write to convey information about something or someone

So, you can see there is a wide range of options or genres of writing to choose from. If you feel inspired by the work you have been doing for Critical Reading, for instance, you might want to try your own hand at writing a poem, a short story or a piece of dramatic script. Or maybe you have enjoyed studying the techniques used by the writers of the RUAE passages and you would like to write something personal, reflective, persuasive or argumentative. Alternatively, you may want to put your energy into writing a review or report on a sporting, musical or other cultural event, or maybe you would like to write a biographical piece about a person.

There are many options, so take some time to consider carefully what to choose. There is no doubt that writing is hard work for everybody, but if you can choose a topic or idea that genuinely interests you, you will find the motivation and enthusiasm to produce your best piece of writing so far.

Portfolio writing key data

Your first main decision	Broadly creative or broadly discursive
Your second main decision	Choose sub-genre
Word limit	1,000 words – but bibliography and title do not count towards this limit
Total number of marks available	Marked out of 15 but scaled up to 30 marks
Percentage of the total marks available for National 5 English	30%

Portfolio Writing: How to do it

This section of the book covers success criteria for portfolio writing, advice for portfolio writing in the genres of persuasive writing, reflective writing and prose fiction, and examples pieces or 'model answers' in these three genres.

For many people working towards National 5 English, the writing of the portfolio piece is one of the most interesting and satisfying parts of the course. Remember, the portfolio is sent off for external assessment and makes up 30% of your final grade – so it is clearly important to invest plenty of time and energy into producing the very best piece you can write. The writing portfolio gives you the opportunity to be creative, to explore areas that are of interest to you personally and to work hard at crafting your own piece of writing.

The three model pieces which follow are to be used as examples only, and must not be reproduced in any way, either fully or in part. You should study them to consider the planning, structure and techniques used by the writer in each case.

The topics and themes of your own writing will be different from the topics and themes covered in these examples. The fact that the portfolio piece is personal to you is one of the most appealing aspects of National 5 English – you can write about topics or in genres that genuinely interest and excite you.

1 | *Success criteria for portfolio writing*

Discursive writing

There are four main things that you should aim to do if you choose to work on a piece of discursive writing.

1. Focus your writing on the topic in hand. Choose relevant, well-researched points and information.
2. Set your ideas out carefully – your essay needs to be convincing. If your purpose is to persuade the reader, then your essay must be persuasive.
3. Use a variety of interesting language and vocabulary. Make deliberate choices about the literary techniques you want to employ.
4. Plan and organise your work so that its structure adds to the impact of what you are saying.

Creative writing

There are four main things that you should aim to do if you choose to work on a piece of creative writing.

1. You must show creativity; your work must have interesting, creative ideas.
2. If you are writing a reflective essay, you must express your feelings and reactions to experiences or changing circumstances. If you can do this with sensitivity, insight and self-awareness, you will do well.

3. You must employ features of the genre or literary techniques. You must vary your language and vocabulary.
4. You must think of ways to use the structure of your writing to enhance its impact.

2   *Advice for portfolio writing*

Whatever the purpose of the piece of writing you are working on, it is always useful to remember that you must engage your reader. Even in persuasive or argumentative writing, you need to include some colourful language, or a little creative flair, to arouse your reader's interest in the topic and to persuade them to consider your point of view. So, creativity is important whether you have opted for the discursive or the creative option.

Write carefully and accurately. Aim to write reasonably quickly but take time every so often to read and re-read what you have written. It doesn't hurt to become just a little obsessive about this; ask yourself if you have used the best possible word, or if you have phrased something in the best possible way. Ask yourself if there is anything better that can be done with punctuation, word choice or imagery. Be meticulous and precise in your writing and take pride in what you are producing.

Transfer your skills from the RUAE and Critical Reading parts of the course. Think of the language, literary devices and linguistic features that you have been reading about and commenting on in the work of professional writers. Can you transfer any of these features into your own writing? Can you come up with a startlingly fresh and interesting metaphor? Is there a particularly effective word that you have come across that will bring a line of your creative writing to life? Are there interesting aspects of sentence structure or punctuation that you can employ to create effects? Or can you learn from the paragraph structure of a reading passage how to build an argument that will persuade your reader? How do professional writers start into their topics in ways which engage their readers? And how do they finish and conclude their pieces? How do they 'leave' their readers?

Checklist for your draft portfolio piece:

1. Have I included an interesting metaphor or simile? ☐
2. Have I worked hard to ensure my word choice is interesting and varied? ☐
3. Have I used any interesting features of sentence structure or punctuation? ☐
4. Have I thought about the structure of my paragraphs? ☐
5. Have I started my writing in a way that engages the reader? ☐
6. Have I concluded my writing in a thought-provoking way? ☐

Choose topics for writing that draw on your enthusiasm and experience. This goes for persuasive or argumentative writing as well as creative writing. If there is a topic or an issue about which you feel strongly or passionately, you are more likely to persuade your reader. It is also more likely that you will know people who you can talk to about your topic as part of your research. Likewise, if you write a story that is set in a place you know well, your descriptions are more likely to be realistic and convincing.

Discursive writing topics

Try to come up with some potential topics for an argumentative or discursive writing piece. The topics could be local, national or international issues.

- **Local examples:** a local issue such as transport, facilities for young people or help for disadvantaged young people. For example, is there sufficient support for young carers in your area? What is going on within your town or local authority area that affects young people? Are there good employment or educational opportunities? What about transport and leisure facilities? Is your local area a good place for young people to live? You may have to work hard to gather information on local topics, but talking to or interviewing people can help.

- **National examples:** are there political or other national issues affecting young people in Scotland or the UK? What is being done to tackle inequalities related to wealth and poverty at Scottish or UK levels? Do you think enough is being done? Is it being done fairly? Are education systems fair and equitable for everyone? What about college and university opportunities? What about employment opportunities for young people?

- **International or geopolitical topics:** are there international or geopolitical topics that interest you? Are there international topics that are especially interesting to young people? These would include 'big picture' topics such as globalisation, the climate emergency, digital developments, or international politics and power. These topics can be complex, with a great deal of information and data available, but you may find something that really captures your imagination.

Creative writing topics

Complete the following short tasks. You may find that you are enjoying responding to one of these tasks, and it could lead on to the beginnings of a longer piece of work. Work quickly, giving yourself 10 or 15 minutes for each task. Don't edit your work and try not to pause; just write, and you will be less likely to be self-critical or to allow doubts to arise about what you are writing.

- Write 150 words from the point of view of an invented character – contemporary or historic.
- Describe an interesting place you know very well in 150 words. You could use this as a starter point for a fictional story.
- Write a description 150 words long about an imaginary setting. This could be a fantasy setting, a futuristic setting or a historical setting.
- Describe a scene from a photograph you remember well in precise detail, using about 150 words. You may decide the description of the photograph is good enough to use as the starting point for a piece of reflective writing.

When you are working on your portfolio piece, you should train yourself to think about your writing in quiet moments outside of class time. If you begin to enjoy planning your work, or thinking of words or images to use, your writing can begin to take a life of its own. As with any creative project – such as writing music, choreographing a dance or painting a picture – the work can become exciting, interesting and deeply satisfying.

TOP TIP

Write what you know! You are much more likely to write well and to write convincingly if you choose a discursive topic that is close to your heart, or if you set a piece of fiction in a place you know well.

Renewable Revolution

Nou Thunneran Thor's gowff-baa's tee'd up at Dounreay.
He'll swipe it yet
a gode-like dunt wi Odin's borrowed brassie ...
Whit a fricht he'll get!

Robert Garioch – from 'Thor's Oh!'

An orange stain of rust is spreading across the iconic white cooling dome of the nuclear reactor at Dounreay, in Caithness. The stain may be a fitting symbol for the demise of nuclear power in Scotland.

In the beginning, in the nineteen fifties, nuclear power was hailed as the answer to all of our energy needs. A by-product of weapons research during WW2, this tremendous new power source was going to be too cheap to meter. It would keep us warm, light our homes and power our appliances forever – for next to nothing. The future looked bright. But now, seventy years on, when Dounreay has come to the end of its productive life and the plant is being decommissioned, many have arrived at a very different view of nuclear power. For them, that unsightly orange stain suggests disrepair, decay and pollution.

Nuclear power has had a chequered history across the world. While the UK, France and Germany have reasonably good safety records, other developed nations have a shameful record of major incidents. The worst accident in the United States happened in 1979, when the reactor at Three Mile Island in Pennsylvania overheated, and 150,000 litres of toxic radioactive wastewater had to be dumped in the Susquehanna River. The incident cost a billion dollars to clean up. Then, in 1986, came the Chernobyl catastrophe in the former Soviet Union. This horrendous nuclear explosion resulted in a vast cloud raining radioactive material over much of Western Europe. Chernobyl is thought to be responsible for thousands of cancer deaths, and cost 18 billion roubles. It remains the world's worst nuclear disaster.

Most recently, the appalling Fukushima disaster in Japan in 2011 may yet prove to be the final nail in the coffin for the nuclear industry. How will people ever forget those terrifying TV pictures of the Fukushima plant blowing up? Although the Fukushima explosions were the result of an earthquake and a tsunami, the dreadful pollution following the incident has convinced many that the nuclear industry is not safe, and that nuclear power can never be truly clean. Many nations are now turning their backs on the technology. Most prominently, Germany has completely abandoned new nuclear power stations in favour of renewable technologies. Austria, Italy and Sweden have already phased out, or are in the process of phasing out, nuclear power.

Yet there are still those who insist that nuclear power is the only way forward to meet the UK's growing demands for cheap energy. Worryingly, both the UK and France have committed to a new generation of nuclear power plants, with UK energy minister Charles Henry announcing recently that 'Plans for the first new nuclear power station to begin generating electricity by 2018 remain on course.' Apart from the dreadful track record the international nuclear industry has for safety, I'm particularly concerned about what will be done with the tonnes of toxic waste belching out of these new nuclear power stations. Reactors currently in operation in the UK will produce an estimated 36,590 cubic metres of waste material, which will remain hazardous for thousands of years. Humans haven't yet invented a material that can store these deadly toxins and sludges safely for this length of time. Caithness residents know all too well about the routine, periodic discovery of radioactive 'particles' on Sandside Beach, by the Dounreay plant. In fact, brief TV news items about discoveries like this at Dounreay are so common that we have become desensitised to them.

I spoke to one local man who has worked in the Dounreay plant about his views on the nuclear industry in the UK. 'I always felt that Dounreay was safe. I always felt safe working there', says Sinclair MacKay, a retired engineer. 'I think the UK has some of the best safety regimes in the world. And nuclear power is relatively cheap, and it doesn't release a lot of carbon.' But what does he think about the problem of the long-term storage of waste? 'That is a real problem, and a problem that we don't have with renewable energy sources.'

Happily, Caithness, like the rest of Scotland, looks like it will avoid new nuclear power stations. The Scottish Government has no plans to build new nuclear facilities. Dounreay will rust in peace. And Caithness is now at the forefront of the renewables revolution. Not everyone loves renewable technology. Wind farms in particular have attracted their fair share of opposition from groups opposed to their visual impact. The John Muir Trust, for example, would very much like to see wind development limited in the wide, wild spaces of the Highlands. Local Caithness groups have worked hard to try to block commercial wind developments such as those at Reay, Spittal and Camster.

For me, the visual impact of wind turbines is much less of an issue than nuclear waste is. Visual impact is just something we are going to have to learn to live with. The sight of the gigantic turbines from the eerie, neolithic Camster Cairns is a weird juxtaposition, but somehow fascinating. And I think the view to the south of the magnificent mountains of Morven and Scaraben with wind turbines rotating elegantly in the foreground is a real symbol of modernity and progress. Smaller farm and domestic turbines are enabling businesses and householders to generate their own clean energy across Scotland, and Caithness and the Highlands will certainly benefit in the future from the development of offshore marine renewables in the Pentland and Moray Firths. As one politician has said, Scotland could become 'the Saudi Arabia of renewables'.

Governments around the world should turn their backs on nuclear power now. There have simply been too many disasters in the past, and the problems with the disposal of waste are simply too great for us to go ahead with new nuclear plants. Instead, we should put all our efforts into developing renewable energy technologies that are clean, sustainable and affordable. What's not to like about the renewable future?

Bibliography:

BBC News – Guide to Nuclear Power

Caithness Windfarm Information Forum (website)

John Muir Trust (website)

Wikipedia pages on Chernobyl, Three Mile Island and Fukushima

World Nuclear News (online newspaper)

Interviews:

Mr. S. MacKay, retired engineer.

Ms. D. Waugh, physics teacher.

Commentary on *Renewable Revolution*

This argumentative essay begins with a colourful and relevant quote from the poet Robert Garioch. The quote uses the image of the god Thor striking the reactor dome like a golf ball – suggesting that the nuclear reactor is dangerous and could blow up.

> ### Candidate question
>
> *Is it OK to use a quote from a poem or a creative source in my discursive writing?*
>
> **A** Yes, it is. Short quotes from creative literature can help to add colour to a discursive piece, and if they are well chosen, they can enhance your line of argument.

The first paragraph of the essay then begins with a clear image that readers can visualise – that of the reactor dome itself.

The writer is a young person from the Highlands, and the topic is well chosen because it has both local and international dimensions. Energy has been generated in the writer's area in different ways, and the essay goes on to consider which of these would be the best option for the future. The essay has a clear, powerful anti-nuclear stance.

This writer has made the most of community links, interviewing a local man who has professional expertise in the subject, and a teacher – bringing a cross-curricular dimension to the writing. We get the strong sense that the writer is genuinely interested in science and energy policy.

 KEY CONCEPTS

Stance simply means the writer's attitude or point of view towards the topic being discussed/written about.

> ### Candidate question
>
> *Should I interview someone as part of my research for discursive writing?*
>
> **A** Interviewing someone in your community is one really good way of developing your knowledge of the topic and will almost certainly enhance your writing.

The piece has been well-researched. The writer has used three relevant and reputable websites and has read two online articles. The writer has shown initiative by interviewing people; this is a really good way to learn about a topic, and to bring other expert voices or quotes into the essay.

The language used is both creative and persuasive. The essay begins with the symbol of the decaying reactor cooling dome. The writer uses three-part structures for persuasive effect – 'keep us warm, light our homes and power our appliances' – and chooses powerful, emotive words like 'shameful', 'toxic' and 'horrendous'. The essay includes a pun ('rust in peace') and uses some alliteration and wordplay in the title *Renewable Revolution* – the word 'revolution' could mean a complete change or could refer to the revolving blades of the wind turbines.

Is it acceptable to use the word 'I' in a piece of discursive or argumentative writing?

 Yes, it is acceptable occasionally to use the word 'I' in writing like this, because this genre of writing is written from your personal point of view.

In terms of structure, the piece is simple but effective. It covers nuclear history, nuclear problems, the interview and renewable alternatives. The conclusion is brief but punchy and sums up the argument neatly in a final rhetorical question: 'What's not to like about the renewable future?'

Assessment focus points	Examples in piece
Features of the argumentative genre deployed effectively?	Yes. Colourful but factual and well researched, builds argument against nuclear power covering a series of different aspects. Scientific reading and research have informed this piece.
Language is varied and used to create particular effects?	Yes. Quoted poetry, imagery and descriptions of landscape all bring colour to the piece without detracting from overall focus and purpose to persuade reader of writer's point of view.
Structure of the piece enhances purpose/meaning?	Yes. An arresting and intriguing opening, followed by clearly structured paragraphs covering different sub-topics to do with energy policy. Argument builds as piece goes on, and piece concludes with persuasive question.

Example Portfolio Writing – Creative (personal/reflective)

Diamond

Going to a metal gig at the Glasgow Barrowlands was always an indescribable thrill for me. The finest, loudest and heaviest of bands would come from all over the world, relishing the chance to perform for the legendary Barrowlands crowd. A Glaswegian warmth exuded from the weird and ugly assortment of leather-clad metalheads who packed the seedy, sticky-floored, low-roofed venue. Flat beer spilled from plastic pint beakers. The house lights went down. The support band struck up. The stink of the crowd was awesome, and disgusting. Steam rose from the bodies and mingled above them. The stink of a metal crowd. Part of that stink was you, and you were part of it. You were part of that diabolical, magical crowd.

I was 18 years old when I saw Pantera at the Barrowlands in 1992. They were the biggest thing in metal that year: progressive, aggressive, loud, energetic, melodic, thrilling. Phil Anselmo, the singer, was a sleek skinhead panther who roared in tune but looked like he should be locked up in jail. Even better than Anselmo for me, though, was seeing Diamond Darrell, Pantera's lead guitar player. I spotted him before the band took to the stage. I was at the front of the floor, the house lights were back on, and he was behind the drum riser tuning his guitar. If Anselmo looked like a panther, Darrell was distinctly leonine in his appearance. A great frizzy mane of red hair stuck out from his head in all directions, and his long red beard jutted out from his chin like rusty wire wool. He was a strong-looking, well-built young man, and he sported a guitar with a sharp, angular design. The guitar was newly strung and the silvery string ends sprung out from the headstock. I called his name and he turned to me with a wide grin and gave a wide, friendly wave. Diamond Darrell exuded a natural warmth.

Pantera swaggered out on to the stage. The Barras went mental. The volume and energy of the performance were immense. The crowd surged like a single living organism – sweating, steaming, jumping, roaring. Performers and audience were one. (They had allowed little kids into the licensed venue for the first time ever that night. I thought it was cute the way they gaped wide-eyed from their perches on their dads' shoulders, awestruck at the magnificent and slightly frightening spectacle before them.) Respite from the intense heat, the stifling stench and the violent jostling of the crowd came only when you broke the surface to surf the crowd on the hands of the other fans. For a few precious, cool seconds you could see everything, everyone could see you, and Diamond Darrell was on the very lip of the stage, thrashing at those new strings, grinning at you, showering the crowd with machine-gun, staccato chords, or a soaring solo break. It was greater than diabolical: it was heavenly, transcendent.

*   *   *

Diamond Darrell was shot dead in Ohio in December 2004. A disgruntled, crazed fan blamed him for the break-up of Pantera and took things to this insane extreme. When I heard the news, I felt an immediate, profound sadness. I guess I hadn't listened to Pantera for years, but the experience of being a part of the crowd and of making that small personal connection to him had stayed with me at a deep level. I dug out my old albums and thought about this vibrant young talent, gunned down in his prime, doing what he loved best. The world of rock went into mourning. Tributes poured into the metal websites. The man's popularity was astonishing in its scale, but not astonishing to those of us who had been touched by his energy and his charisma. He left the world a duller, stiller, quieter place.

Commentary on *Diamond*

This writer has chosen a good topic. The writer is clearly a metal fan, and loves the genre, and the characters of the musicians who play it. If you opt to write a personal or reflective essay, your own enthusiasms will be very important in selecting a topic that is right for you.

The title has been carefully considered. Although simple, it contains the artist's name, and has clear, direct connotations of value and worth.

The opening of the essay is atmospheric and conveys the writer's fascination – and also a sense of revulsion – at the scene. The writing is sensual, focusing on the smells of the venue, and including small details like the beer being spilled or the sticky floor.

The writing is consciously creative. Remember that, although the genre is called 'personal' or 'reflective', it remains a creative task.

There are contrasts – 'the lights went down, the support band struck up' – and there is a paradox – 'diabolical, magical crowd'. The images used to describe the musicians are slightly over the top – maybe deliberately so. This is in keeping with the genre of music journalism and particularly writing about the genres of rock or metal. So, the singer is described as a 'panther' and the guitarist as 'leonine', with a 'mane of red hair'. The images themselves begin to provide some reflection. The musicians clearly had a powerful effect on this young music fan; they seem very impressive, almost frightening.

The writing conveys a reflective sense of belonging between the writer and the other fans, especially in the image comparing the crowd to 'a single, living organism'. The writer uses colloquialisms in the phrase 'The Barras went mental'. This is acceptable when done deliberately in a creative piece like this and gives us a sense of the writer's own 'voice'. Although the task is called a 'reflective essay', this doesn't mean that the language needs to be excessively formal.

TOP TIP

Remember that, even if you are writing in the personal, reflective, discursive or argumentative genre, the task still requires creativity. Just because you aren't writing poetry, prose fiction or drama doesn't mean you can't be creative!

Candidate question

Is it really OK to use colloquial language for an English portfolio piece?

A Yes, it is, as long as you are in control and want to use colloquial language to create a particular effect. In this piece, the colloquial language helps to give a sense of the writer's 'voice'.

In terms of structure, this piece has been very carefully planned to create a powerful impact at the end. The last line of the second-last paragraph describes Diamond Darrell on stage, in the very prime of his life. The essay then moves with swift drama into the final paragraph, which begins with devastating bluntness – 'Diamond Darrell was shot dead ...'. This is what is meant by using structure to assist impact. The paragraph structure makes the information seem all the more shocking.

This essay uses a true story and a very sad, dramatic and tragic event to provide a context for some poignant reflection. After describing so much energy and noise, the essay ends on a very quiet note – 'a duller,

TOP TIP

If you are able to effectively use the structure of your writing to enhance dramatic or other effects, this can help you to achieve a higher mark.

stiller, quieter place'. We get the sense that the writer is thinking deeply and reflecting at the close of the essay, but the reflection is also built right the way through the piece – in its celebration of Diamond Darrell while he was alive.

Assessment focus points	Examples in piece
Features of the reflective/ personal genre deployed effectively?	Yes. Piece gives sense of genuine personal involvement and participation. Appropriate tone – not too formal, but accurate and lively, personal and reflective communication.
Language is varied and used to create particular effects?	Yes. Creativity in imagery ('leonine' and 'panther'). Effective mood and scene-setting around sights, sounds and smells. Arresting and intriguing title with symbolic suggestive power.
Structure of the piece enhances purpose/meaning?	Yes. Particularly with regard to shocking, tragic ending and structure used to communicate this. First part describes the character in life and full of energy, resulting in our shock and sadness as we read of his tragic death.

Swiftly Past the Thieves' Isle

In the final hour of the night we drew swiftly past the Thieves' Isle. Wind and tide were together, moving in the same direction, sweeping us onwards. Everything conspired towards the coming event. Laing was at the helm of the dinghy, broad shoulders and bowed legs. I was curled in the bilge, out of sight. Droplets of brine seeped in between the tarry boards before my face. The dinghy gave a shudder – alive like a horse swimming through the tide whorls – and my entrails turned to water.

Under my fingernails was the black soil of Tafts, where I had drunkenly scratched, sworn and struggled to stay ashore in the night. My hands now were yellow as hens' feet, and I could feel the musket cold in my cold oxter. My breeches were wet, my mouth was dry. Struggling with nausea, I tried to focus on Laing's silhouette as the red glow came up in the East.

His beard jutted out towards the Isle, his other features indistinguishable in the grey dawn light. I could make out his black sea cap under the cold setting moon, and a red smoulder from the bowl of his pipe as he filled his lungs with dregs of smoke. A thick mutter came from the beard, *Keep thee heid below that gunwhale*. I retched up a quarter gill of frothy bile, and spat it weakly into the bilge.

As we rounded the ness into the Bay of Brecks, Laing drew the tiller towards himself, and the dingy lurched in an awkward gybe. The sails relaxed, gave a loud flap and snapped taut again. As the dinghy began to heel over on her opposite side, a scene at once perfectly familiar and yet at the same time completely novel, appeared in my view. On the shore, the red sandstone of the Hall of Brecks glowed in the dawn light, as it did every morning. The light winked in the thirteen glass-paned windows of the facade. The little signal cannon sat as always by the top of the steps down to the sunken garden.

But in the bay was anchored a timber structure comparable in size to the Hall; a naval ship of such magnitude and intimidating grandeur that I somehow imagined it to be like a floating Hall, riding at anchor in the bay. Her cannon hatches were too many for me to count, but a little signal cannon perched on her quarter deck, just like the signal cannon at the Hall. I could discern the figures of red-coated men with rifles and gleaming bayonets strutting on the deck. A vast, brilliant White Ensign with its crimson cross pulsed with slow regularity in the morning wind. The ensign was as wide as the mainsail of Laing's dinghy.

Was this dreadful ship my destination this October morning, then? She was taller than the hills of the island. Everything about her spoke of power. Poor sinner that I was, I hadn't imagined Laing's contempt for me was such that he would sell me to the Navy without a pang of conscience.

Mister Laing, my voice was a quiet rasp, *Mister Laing, can I have a drink of water?*

I'll give thee a drink of rum, if thu promises to be quiet and sit still.

Rum would be very good indeed, Mister Laing.

He drew a flask from inside his overcoat, unscrewed the top, and held it to my mouth. I would not usually drink rum in the morning. The spirit went inside me, and I tensed to hold it down.

Are you going to sell me to them, Sir?

No, Crawford, I don't intend to sell thee. Thee passage on this ship will be two miles oot, and I shall bring thee the two miles back. Just a pilot's service.

Working as a pilot was the only way I had of bringing a few extra guineas home to my poor old Mother at Tafts. Two thin sheep and an ailing Shetland cow were all she would be left with if the Navy took me. The winter had been wet and cold. The damp and the worms had found their way up between the flagstones of the floor. Her meal chest was nearly empty, her peat stack diminished.

A small hope began to glimmer inside me, like the flickering wick of the whale-oil lamp in the byre at Tafts; maybe Laing's intention was to split the pilot's fee, and return me to Tafts. He was much larger and stronger than me, it was true, but he lacked my sea knowledge.

I'll be with thee all the time, he said, *we'll tie the dinghy alongside the warship and I'll tak thee home swiftly on the ebb tide once thu're guided her safely through the Firth. Tak anither sup.*

He handed me the flask and I drank, deeply. The warmth began to return to my body, and my anxiety began to ease. We had come round under the quarter deck of the vast ship into the lee. A rope ladder with hardwood steps clattered over the side and tumbled down forty feet, the last few rungs landed heavily on my head and shoulders, bruising me and concussing me – I think.

Scramble up! said Laing. *I'll tie up and follow thee. Quickly noo!*

Up I went, fool that I was, slipping on the wet rungs, chafing my hands on the hemp of the ropes, my head burning with rum and blows and confused half-thoughts. Then a red sleeve. A rough hand had me by the collar. As I was dragged backwards onto the expansive deck of the ship I heard a heavy thud and a dull metallic slither, as a bag of coins landed in the bottom of Laing's dinghy.

Pleasure dealing with ye, gentlemen!, he called out as he pushed the dinghy off and caught the wind again, *And don't worry, Crawford: I'll tak care o thee mither!*

Commentary on *Swiftly Past the Thieves' Isle*

One of the great joys of writing stories or fiction is that there is a limitless amount of choice – in terms of characters, setting and events. You can invent whatever you want to and focus on things that interest you and appeal to you.

This writer is clearly interested in history and has chosen to write a short piece of historical fiction. This is just one genre of fiction, and it may be that you are interested in writing fantasy, science fiction, crime fiction or some other genre that appeals to you.

The title of this story is a phrase taken from the story itself – authors will often do this, to set readers thinking about the significance of the phrase from the beginning.

There are only two characters in this story (apart from the brief mention of the narrator's mother and the sailor who pulls him aboard the warship). Short stories need to be simple, and keeping the number of characters small is important. The events of the story are reasonably straightforward, too. This story focuses on character, description and one main event – simplicity is best.

The first-person narrative allows the writer to create a character – Crawford – who is slightly naïve. It may be that we realise what is happening to him before he does. A good story always involves problems, and Crawford has a clear and immediate problem – he is being kidnapped. Because it uses a first-person narrative, the story can focus on his physical discomfort and psychological turmoil.

Laing is an ambiguous character – we don't really discover for sure that he is evil until the final stages of the story. The detail of his pipe glowing red in the darkness is certainly sinister, though, and suggests evil.

The setting of this story is on the sea near a Scottish island. It seems as if the writer might know the place, or a place like it. This is important in writing – if you can use a setting that you know, it will be more convincing as fiction. The story is set in the past, possibly in the late eighteenth or early nineteenth century in the times of the 'press gangs' who kidnapped men for the Navy. The story is a bit like some of Robert Louis Stevenson's novel *Kidnapped*, or some of the popular pirate stories or movies that people enjoy. The writer clearly likes history and has used knowledge of history to create a convincing piece of fiction. You might like to think about other areas of your school curriculum for inspiration for your creative writing.

The style of the story is deliberately old-fashioned. The language and the dialogue sound a bit like a nineteenth-century novel. Imagery is appropriate, so the dinghy is compared to a horse swimming, and Crawford's cold hands are compared to 'hens' feet'. Comparisons are used to convey the size of the ship – her flag is as big as the sail of the dinghy, and she is taller than the island hills. A backstory starts to emerge involving Crawford, the farm and his elderly mother.

TOP TIP

If there is a particular sub-genre of fiction that you really enjoy such as science fiction, fantasy literature, horror or dystopian fiction, you may wish to harness your enthusiasm and experiment with writing in this genre for yourself.

KEY CONCEPTS

First-person narrative is when a story is told from the point of view of one of the main characters. First person narrative uses the pronouns 'I' and 'me' to tell the story.

TOP TIP

Make the most of your enthusiasm and knowledge of a subject or topic and 'fictionalise' this knowledge to enhance your short story or novel extract.

The story ends with an ambiguous line of dialogue; we don't know if Laing is making a threat, or if he and Crawford's mother have conspired to trick Crawford. It is a strength in the story that it opens up these different possibilities at the end, rather than concluding too neatly. A short story should end with some form of resolution. The ending of this story resolves Crawford's problem in a way; although he might now be in a very difficult or dangerous situation, he at least knows for sure that Laing has tricked him.

Assessment focus points	Examples in story
Features of the short story genre deployed effectively?	Yes. Small number of characters, one main event, ambiguous ending. Brief but self-contained story. Characterisation achieved in short space of time – Crawford through his thoughts, and Laing through actions, associations and speech.
Language is varied and used to create particular effects?	Yes. Told from first-person point of view with lots of precise sensory details. Effective imagery – dinghy compared to horse, etc. Some old-style archaic language for effect: guineas, breeches, etc.
Structure of the piece enhances purpose/meaning?	Yes. Opens directly into action; fills in some backstory, and concludes with further action, a shocking surprise and some ongoing uncertainty.

Glossary

Adjective – a word that describes a noun.

Alliteration/alliterative – repetition of the same consonants, usually to highlight what is being said.

Analyse – to examine in detail in order to discover meaning, essential features, etc.

Anaphora – the repetition of a word or phrase at the beginning of successive phrases or sentences.

Assonance – repetition of similar vowel sounds to create an effect similar to rhyme or to highlight (usually the tone) what is being said.

Bibliography – a list of books or other material on a subject.

Clause – a unit of sense below the level of a sentence.

Climax – a significant or dramatic final point.

Colloquial – language of everyday speech.

Compound sentence – a sentence containing at least two coordinate clauses.

Conjunction – a word that joins together or connects other words, phrases, clauses (but, and, or).

Connotation – whatever a word suggests (rather than means).

Connote – suggest.

Contradiction – a combination of two terms that oppose each other.

Contrast – two ideas, words or images that appear opposite or very different but which together reveal an underlying significance.

Convey – to cause information or feelings to be known or understood by someone.

Dramatic – relating to drama – striking, exciting.

Dramatic monologue – a poem told in the first person, in which the speaker reveals aspects of their character.

Ellipsis – a sequence of three dots (...) indicating an omission in text.

Emphasis – special or extra importance that is given to an activity or to a part or aspect of something.

Enjambment – where a sentence runs on over two or more lines of a poem. (Also known as a 'run-on line'.)

First-person narration – where a character or speaker uses 'I' or 'me'.

Genre – a particular type of literature, painting, music, film, or other art form which people consider as a class because it has special characteristics.

Humour – words or phrases which amuse in order to make a point.

Hyperbole – the use of exaggeration for heightened effect.

Image/imagery – mental picture of an idea or object.

Imply – to express or indicate by a hint; suggest

Impression – an effect produced in the mind by a stimulus; sensation

Internal rhyme – rhyming words within lines of poetry.

Irony/ironical – stating the opposite of what is meant to make a significant point.

Italic – a cursive font (italic).

Juxtaposition – the placing of words, images or ideas side by side.

Listing – series of items usually separated by commas or by conjunctions.

Literal root – the real object, person, idea etc. being described in a simile or metaphor.

Literary technique – any aspect of the writer's craft, including, but not limited to, devices such as imagery, word choice, characterisation, irony, sentence structure, etc.

Metaphor – a device of comparison, saying one thing is something else.

Minor sentence – a sentence without a main verb or a main subject.

Monosyllabic – of one syllable.

Mood – a predominant or pervading feeling, spirit, or tone.

Motif – a distinctive idea, esp a theme elaborated on in a piece of music, literature, etc.

Onomatopoeia - using a word which sounds the same as the sound of the thing it names.

Paradox - words, phrases, images or ideas that seem to contradict each other.

Paraphrase - to put (something) into other words; restate (something).

Persona - the speaker in a poem.

Personification - ascribing human qualities to inanimate objects.

Perspective - point of view.

Plosive - A consonant sound such as 'b' or 'p', made by the sudden release of breath.

Poetry - literature in metrical form; verse.

Prose - ordinary written language, in contrast to poetry.

Punctuation - the use of symbols such as full stops or periods, commas, or question marks to divide written words into sentences and clauses.

Reiterate - to say or do again or repeatedly.

Repetition - words, phrases or expressions repeated for emphasis or dramatic effect.

Rhetorical question - a question that implies its own answer.

Rhyme - words with the same or similar sounds, often at the end of lines of poetry.

Rhythm - a repeated pattern of stressed sound, although the repetition does not have to be regular.

Setting - the place or time in which a literary text such as a play or novel, or a scene in a film, takes place.

Sibilant - the soft 's', 'c' and 'z' sounds.

Simile - a device of comparison, saying one thing is like something else, using the word 'like' or 'as'.

Stanza - one of the parts into which a poem is divided.

Structure - the way in which something is made, built, or organised.

Symbolism/symbol - the use of an object to represent something else.

Synonym - a word or expression which means the same as another word or expression.

Syntax - the ways that words can be put together, or are put together, in order to make sentences.

Theme - an important idea or subject that runs through a piece of writing.

Tone - the feeling of a piece of writing that conveys the writer's attitude to the subject matter.

Topic sentence - a sentence in a paragraph that expresses the main idea or point of the whole paragraph.

Verse - a stanza or other short subdivision of a poem or song

Word choice - a word or words used for their connotative meaning and effect.

Index

A

adjective, 173
alliteration/alliterative, 173
All That Glisters (Anne Donovan), 106-107, 115-117
analyse, 15, 173
anaphora, 173
anticlimax, 24
argument, 6
assonance, 173

B

baby seals, 19
bibliography, 155, 173
Black Watch (Gregory Burke), 78-79, 81, 145-146
Burns, Robert, 64

C

Celtic Connections, 13, 49-50
The Chair, 49-50
clauses, 25, 173
climate change and poverty, 26, 29, 32-34
climax, 173
colloquial, 173
colon (:), 25
comical, 64
commands, 24
comma or commas, 25
commonality, 70-71
complex sentence, 25
compound sentence, 25, 173
conclusion, 38-41
    approach to answering questions, 38-39
    building skills for, 39-40, 80
    consolidation of learning, 40, 80
    effectiveness of, 41
    writing, 79-80
conjunction, 173
connotation, 173
contradiction, 173
contrast, 173
contrasting types of sentences, 25
convey, 173
coral reefs, 26-28, 33

creative writing, 156, 158-161
    Diamond, 166-168
    Swiftly Past the Thieves' Isle, 169-172
critical essay, 64-65
    assessment for, 65
    building skills for, 75-76
    consolidation of learning, 76
    questions for drama, prose and poetry, 75
    success criteria for, 75
critical reading, 63, 66
    approach, 67-74
    building skills for, 68-70
    consolidation of learning, 69
    tips and advice on, 81-82

D

Danny Kyle Open Stage award, 50
Death in a Nut (Duncan Williamson), 108-110, 118-119
discursive writing, 156, 158
    international or geopolitical topics, 160
    local examples, 160
    national examples, 160
    Renewable Revolution, 162-165
drama, 66
    model question and answers, 83-100
dramatic monologue, 173
dramatic script, 66, 173
Duck Feet (Ely Percy), 104-105, 113-114

E

Egg Terrorists, 35, 56-62
ellipsis, 30, 173
emphasis, 173
enjambment, 73, 173
essay planning, 78-79
    building skills for, 79
    consolidation of learning, 79
examples of language, 31

F

Federer, Roger, 42

fiction, 66
first-person narration, 173

G

'Gap Year' (Jackie Kay), 125-126, 136-139
genre, 66, 173
Get Myself Connected, 13, 34, 49-55
Glasgow, 49
granite boulders, 19
group discussion, 151, 154

H

Henman, Tim, 42
higher order thinking, 82
humour, 173
hyperbole, 173

I

image/imagery, 19-24, 173
    building skills, 20-22
    consolidation of learning, 21-22
    figurative extension, 19
    'figurative extension' of, 19
    'literal root' of image, 19
imply/implication, 15, 22-23, 31, 35, 173
impression, 173
internal rhyme, 173
introduction, writing, 76-77
    building skills for, 76
    consolidation of learning, 77
irony/ironical, 173
italic, 173

J

Just Grow Up!, 26, 35, 42-48
juxtaposition, 173

K

killer whales, 19, 21

L

light-hearted, 64
links/linking between topics and ideas, 32, 34

building skills, 32–33
consolidation of learning, 33–34
listing, 24, 173
literal root, 23, 173
literary technique, 173
'Little Girls' (Len Pennie), 129–130, 142–144
long sentences, 24
'Love' (Edwin Morgan), 127–128, 140–141

M
McEnroe, John, 42
'Medusa' (Carol Ann Duffy), 120–122, 131–132
metaphor, 19–21, 23, 173
minor sentences, 25, 173
monosyllabic, 173
mood, 64, 173
motif, 173
Murray, Andy, 22–23, 42–43

N
novels, 66

O
'Old Highland Woman' (Norman MacCaig), 123–124, 133–135
onomatopoeia, 174

P
paradox, 174
paragraph, 64
paraphrase, 14, 174
persona, 174
personification, 23, 174
perspective, 174
plays, 66
plosive, 174
poetry, 66, 174
model question and answers, 120–144
portfolio writing, 155
advice for, 159–160
approach to, 158–159
creative, 156, 158–159
discursive, 156, 158
positive impression, 18
power of three, 26
prose, 66, 174
model question and answers, 101–119
punctuation, 25, 174

Q
question papers, example and model, 42–62
quotations, 81

R
Reading for Understanding, Analysis and Evaluation (RUAE), 6–7
examination question paper for, 7
reiterate, 174
relaxed or foreboding, 64
repetition, 174
rhetorical question, 24, 26, 30, 174
rhyme, 174
rhythm, 174

S
Sailmaker (Alan Spence), 87–89, 96–97
Scottish literary text, 63–64
building skills for, 71–73
commonest question type in, 67
consolidation of learning, 72
drama model question and answers, 83–100
eight-mark question, 70–71
examples of language' questions and 'summarise' questions, 67–68
poetry model question and answers, 120–144
prose model question and answers, 101–119
success criteria, 67
Scottish music, 34
semicolon (;), 25
sentence structure, 23–31, 40
building skills, 27–30
consolidation of learning, 28, 30
key features of, 24–27
setting, 174
short sentences, 24
short stories, 66
sibilant, 174
simile, 20, 22–23, 174
simple sentence, 25
sinister, 64
soul-crushing poverty, 33–34
spoken language, 151–154
stance, 164
stanzas, 66, 174

statements, 24
The Strange Case of Dr Jekyll and Mr Hyde (Robert Louis Stevenson), 101–103, 111–112
structure, 174
submarines, 19
summarising/summary question, 35–38
building skills, 36
consolidation of learning, 37
symbolism/symbol, 174
synonym, 13, 174
syntax/word order, 24, 174

T
Tally's Blood (Ann Marie Di Mambro), 90–92, 98–100
tense, 64
thematic links, 73
theme or themes of literary text, 65, 174
three-part structures, 26
To Kill a Mockingbird (Harper Lee), 65, 78–79, 147–148
tone, 174
topic sentences, 174
building skills for, 77
consolidation of learning, 78
'Trio' (Edwin Morgan), 78–79, 149–150
'Trouble is not my middle name' (Liz Lochhead), 68

U
'using your own words' questions, 9–14

V
verse, 64, 66, 174

W
'We lost us for a while' (Robert Alan Jamieson), 71, 73
word choice, 24, 174
building skills, 16
connotations, 15
consolidation of learning, 17
protection of wild birds, 17–18
single word quotation, 15

Y
Yellow Moon (David Greig), 83–86, 93–95